8.99

SOUP

RECIPES AND TEXT
DIANE ROSSEN WORTHINGTON

GENERAL EDITOR
CHUCK WILLIAMS

PHOTOGRAPHS
NOEL BARNHURST

APPLE

CONTENTS

SUMMER SOUPS

WINTER SOUPS

CHICKEN SOUPS

INTRODUCTION

A cold winter afternoon is the moment you might think to make a pot of hearty soup. But there's no reason to limit yourself. Soup can be the perfect meal at so many different times: A chilled fruit soup refreshes on a July afternoon, a puréed vegetable soup makes a quick and satisfying weeknight supper, or a refined seafood bisque sets the tone for a formal dinner party. In this cookbook, you will find recipes that will inspire you to make soup whenever the mood strikes—there's even a chapter of chicken soups from around the world.

Each recipe in this book is kitchen-tested and highlights a particular ingredient, term, or cooking technique that is used in the soup. A chapter of basics in the back of the book offers an overview of soup making, with recipes for homemade stocks and all the other information you'll need. Just take a look through these pages, and I believe you'll be ready to take out the soup pot at once!

THE CLASSICS

Certain soups have earned a reputation as classic soups, distinctive preparations that have graced the table for as long as cooks can remember. Included here are eight such culinary standard-bearers, now enjoyed far beyond their places of origin.

CHICKEN NOODLE SOUP

In a large saucepan over medium-high heat, bring the stock to a simmer. Add the chicken breast and simmer just until tender and no trace of pink remains, 8–10 minutes. Remove from the heat and let the chicken cool in the liquid. Transfer the chicken to a cutting board and cut into 1-inch (2.5-cm) cubes. Set aside.

Return the chicken stock to a simmer over medium-high heat and add the onion, carrots, and celery. Simmer until the vegetables are slightly softened, about 10 minutes, skimming away any foam that rises to the surface of the stock.

Add the cubed chicken, noodles, 2 tablespoons of the parsley, and salt and pepper to taste. Simmer until the noodles are tender, about 3 minutes.

Ladle the soup into warmed bowls and sprinkle with the remaining 1 tablespoon parsley. Serve immediately.

MAKES 4 SERVINGS

DICING ONIONS

Here is a method that makes dicing onions easy. Slice off both ends of the onion and peel it. Stand the onion on its root end and make a series of slices just down to, but not through, the root end. Give the onion a quarter turn and make another series of slices across the first set of slices, again not cutting all the way through. Move the knife back to the center cut and slice the onion in half through the root. Lay each onion half flat side down on the cutting board and cut across the slices to make dice.

6 cups (48 fl oz/1.5 l) chicken stock (page 110) or prepared broth

1 skinless, boneless whole chicken breast, about ½ lb (250 g)

1 yellow onion, finely diced

2 carrots, peeled, halved lengthwise, and thinly sliced

2 celery stalks, thinly sliced

2 oz (60 g) dried thin egg noodles

3 tablespoons finely chopped fresh flat-leaf (Italian) parsley

Salt and freshly ground pepper

FRENCH ONION SOUP

2 tablespoons vegetable or olive oil

4 large red onions, thinly sliced

¼ teaspoon sugar

4 leeks, including tender green parts, thinly sliced

2 cloves garlic, minced

8 cups (64 fl oz/2 l) beef or chicken stock (page 110) or prepared broth

½ cup (4 fl oz/125 ml) dry white wine

1 bay leaf

½ teaspoon minced fresh thyme or ¼ teaspoon dried thyme

Salt and freshly ground pepper

12 slices baguette, ¼ inch (6 mm) thick

¾ cup (3 oz/90 g) shredded Gruyère or Comté cheese

In a large nonaluminum saucepan over medium-low heat, warm the oil. Add the onions and sauté, stirring occasionally, until wilted, about 15 minutes. Add the sugar and leeks and continue cooking, stirring frequently, until richly colored and caramelized, 30–45 minutes. (You may need to raise the heat to medium to add some color at the end.)

Add the garlic and sauté for 1 minute. Add the stock, wine, bay leaf, and thyme. Cover partially and simmer until the flavors are well blended, about 30 minutes. Season to taste with salt and pepper. Discard the bay leaf.

To serve, preheat the broiler (grill). Ladle the soup into individual flameproof soup bowls. Place 2 or 3 slices of bread on top of each bowl and sprinkle with the cheese. Slide under the broiler about 6 inches (15 cm) from the heat element. Broil until the cheese is bubbly and lightly browned, 3–4 minutes. Serve immediately.

Variation Tip: Beef stock is the traditional stock used for French onion soup. For a lighter version, use chicken stock.

Serving Tip: Serve a simple green salad with this soup for a satisfying light supper.

MAKES 4–6 SERVINGS

CARAMELIZING

This soup's success depends on caramelizing the onions and leeks, a technique that takes time and patience. Caramelization occurs when the sugars naturally present in a vegetable slowly develop a less purely sweet, more complex flavor through long cooking over medium-low or medium heat. Adding a sprinkling of sugar encourages the caramelizing process.

SPLIT PEA SOUP

In a large saucepan over medium heat, warm the oil. Add the onion and sauté until softened, 3–5 minutes. Add the celery and carrots and sauté until just slightly softened, 3 minutes.

Add the split peas, stock, 2 slices of the bacon, parsley, marjoram, and thyme. Reduce the heat to medium-low and bring to a simmer. Cover partially and cook until the peas are tender, 50–60 minutes. Discard the bacon.

Meanwhile, in a frying pan over medium heat, fry the remaining 4 slices bacon until crisp, about 10 minutes. Transfer to paper towels to drain. When cool, crumble and set aside.

Coarsely purée 2 cups (16 fl oz/500 ml) of the soup in a food processor and return the puréed soup to the saucepan. Season with salt and pepper to taste, return the soup to medium heat, and simmer for 5 minutes longer. Taste and adjust the seasoning.

Ladle the soup into warmed bowls and garnish with the crumbled bacon. Serve immediately.

Variation Tip: The crumbled crisp bacon adds a flavorful counterpoint to the creamy split pea flavor. For an alternative garnish, top the soup with chopped honey-baked ham.

Serving Tip: Serve the soup with warm crusty French bread.

MAKES 4 SERVINGS

SPLIT PEAS

Varying in color from pale green to yellow, split peas are best known in their role as the basis for a hearty soup that is synonymous with comfort food. But they can also be boiled and served as a side dish. They result from processing field peas, a variety grown specifically for drying. The skins are removed during the dehydrating, which causes the peas to split in half. A nutritional plus: Dried peas offer about triple the protein found in fresh peas.

1 tablespoon olive oil

1 yellow onion, finely diced

1 celery stalk, thinly sliced

2 small carrots, peeled and thinly sliced

1 cup (7 oz/220 g) dried green or yellow split peas, picked over, rinsed, and drained

4 cups (32 fl oz/1 l) chicken or vegetable stock (pages 110–11) or prepared broth

6 slices bacon

2 tablespoons finely chopped fresh flat-leaf (Italian) parsley

½ teaspoon finely chopped fresh marjoram or ¼ teaspoon dried marjoram

½ teaspoon finely chopped fresh thyme or ¼ teaspoon dried thyme

Salt and freshly ground pepper

NEW ENGLAND
CLAM CHOWDER

3 lb (1.5 kg) littleneck clams in their shells, well scrubbed

1 cup (8 fl oz/250 ml) bottled clam juice or homemade fish stock (page 111)

2 tablespoons unsalted butter

1 yellow onion, finely chopped

½ cup (3 oz/90 g) diced salt pork

2 celery stalks, thinly sliced

2 tablespoons all-purpose (plain) flour

2 waxy red or white potatoes (page 35), about 10 oz (315 g) total weight, diced

3 cups (24 fl oz/750 ml) milk or half-and-half (half cream)

1 bay leaf

Salt and freshly ground white pepper

2 tablespoons finely chopped fresh flat-leaf (Italian) parsley

Chowder crackers for garnish

In a large saucepan over medium-high heat, combine the clams and clam juice and bring to a boil. Reduce the heat to a simmer, cover, and steam the clams until they open, 5–8 minutes. Remove from the heat and discard any clams that failed to open. Remove the clams from their shells (cut in half if very large), reserving a few in the shells for garnish.

Strain the clam juice through a fine-mesh sieve lined with cheese-cloth (muslin) to remove any grit. You should have 1½–2 cups (12–16 fl oz/375–500 ml). Set aside.

In a large saucepan over medium heat, melt the butter. Add the onion and sauté until just softened, 3–5 minutes. Add the salt pork and sauté, stirring occasionally, until the pork is cooked through and the onion is golden brown, about 2 minutes longer. Add the celery and sauté for 1 minute. Add the flour and cook, stirring with a wooden spoon, for 2 minutes longer. Stir in the strained clam juice, potatoes, milk, and bay leaf. Raise the heat to medium-high and bring to a simmer, scraping up any browned bits from the bottom of the pan. Reduce the heat to medium and simmer until the potatoes are tender, about 15 minutes.

Discard the bay leaf and season to taste with salt and white pepper. Add the parsley, shucked clams, and reserved clams in their shells. Cook for 1 minute longer to warm the clams through.

Ladle the chowder into warmed bowls and top with chowder crackers. Serve immediately.

Variation Tip: This chowder includes a bit of flour to thicken the soup base. If you prefer a richer fish flavor, increase the amount of clam juice to taste.

MAKES 4 SERVINGS

SELECTING CLAMS

Always buy clams from a reputable fish merchant. In the case of littlenecks, which are hard-shelled clams, look for even-colored, firm, tightly closed shells. If a shell has opened slightly, tap it; it should immediately close tightly. If it does not, the clam is dead and should be discarded. (Soft-shelled clams, because of a protruding neck, or siphon, do not close as fully when tapped.) Scrub the shells under running water to clean them thoroughly before steaming.

TUSCAN TOMATO SOUP

Preheat the oven to 300°F (150°C). Place the bread slices on a baking sheet and bake until lightly browned, turning once, 10–15 minutes total. Set aside.

In a large soup pot over medium heat, warm the oil. Add the onion and sauté, stirring frequently, until softened, 5–7 minutes. Add the garlic and cook until softened but not browned, about 30 seconds.

Add the tomatoes and stock, raise the heat to high, and bring to a boil. Reduce the heat to medium-low, cover, and cook until the tomatoes are softened, about 30 minutes. Remove from the heat.

In a blender or food processor, purée the soup in batches, leaving a little bit of texture if desired, and return the soup to the pot. Alternatively, process with a handheld blender in the pot until the desired consistency is reached. Return the soup to medium heat and reheat gently. Add the chopped basil and season to taste with salt and pepper.

To serve, place a slice of toasted bread in the bottom of each warmed bowl and sprinkle with a spoonful of Parmesan cheese. Ladle the soup on top and garnish with a basil leaf. Serve it immediately.

MAKES 6–8 SERVINGS

PEELING AND SEEDING TOMATOES

For this soup, select fully sun-ripened tomatoes that are slightly soft to the touch. To peel and seed them, fill a saucepan three-fourths full of water and bring to a boil. Using a sharp knife, score an X in the blossom end of each tomato. In batches, without crowding, immerse the tomatoes in the boiling water and leave for 15–30 seconds, or until the skins just begin to wrinkle. Remove from the pan with a slotted spoon, let cool slightly, then peel away the skins. Cut in half cross-wise and squeeze gently to dislodge the seeds.

6–8 slices French bread, 1 inch (2.5 cm) thick

2 tablespoons extra-virgin olive oil

1 large yellow onion, finely chopped

3 cloves garlic, minced

3 lb (1.5 kg) ripe tomatoes, peeled and seeded *(far left),* then diced

4 cups (32 fl oz/1 l) chicken or vegetable stock (pages 110–11) or prepared broth

½ cup (¾ oz/20 g) finely chopped basil leaves, plus 6–8 whole leaves

Salt and freshly ground pepper

½ cup (2 oz/60 g) freshly grated Parmesan cheese

LENTIL SOUP

2 tablespoons olive oil

1 yellow onion, finely chopped

1 celery stalk, thinly sliced

1 carrot, peeled and thinly sliced

1 clove garlic, minced

1 bay leaf

2 teaspoons curry powder

1 cup (6 oz/185 g) canned diced plum (Roma) tomatoes, with juice

1½ cups (10½ oz/330 g) dried brown or pink lentils, picked over, rinsed, and drained

6 cups (48 fl oz/1.5 l) chicken, beef, or vegetable stock (pages 110–11) or prepared broth

1 lemon, sliced

1 cup (2 oz/60 g) coarsely chopped fresh spinach

Salt and freshly ground pepper

In a large saucepan over medium-high heat, warm the oil. Add the onion, celery, carrot, garlic, and bay leaf and sauté until the vegetables are softened, about 5 minutes. Stir in the curry powder and cook until fragrant, about 1 minute.

Add the tomatoes and their juice, lentils, stock, and lemon slices. Bring to a simmer over medium-high heat. Reduce the heat to medium-low, cover partially, and cook, stirring occasionally, until the lentils are tender, about 30 minutes. Discard the lemon slices and bay leaf.

Just before serving, stir in the spinach, reduce the heat to low, and simmer until the spinach is wilted but still bright green. Season to taste with salt and pepper.

Ladle the soup into warmed bowls and serve immediately.

MAKES 4–6 SERVINGS

LENTIL VARIETIES

Lentils come in a wide range of colors, including brown, green, yellow, red, pink, and ocher. Brown lentils are the type most commonly found in supermarkets, but you could also use pink lentils, what Indian cooks call *masoor dal,* for this recipe, as they cook relatively quickly and break down nicely, becoming a natural thickener for the soup. Although they are pink when uncooked, they turn a pale yellow when cooked. Look for them at Indian markets and natural-food stores.

BEEF CHILI WITH MASA HARINA

In a large nonstick frying pan over medium-high heat, warm 1 tablespoon of the oil. Add half of the beef and cook, stirring occasionally, until browned, 5–7 minutes. Transfer to a colander placed over a bowl to drain off the fat. Repeat with another 1 tablespoon of the oil and the remaining beef. Drain and set aside.

In a large pot over medium heat, warm the remaining 3 tablespoons oil. Add the onions and sauté, stirring occasionally, until softened, 5–7 minutes. Add the garlic and sauté for 1 minute. Add the jalapeño, chili powder, cumin, oregano, and coriander, stir until well combined, and cook for 1 minute longer.

Add the reserved beef, the beer, stock, and tomatoes and bring to a gentle simmer. Reduce the heat to medium-low, cover, and simmer, stirring occasionally, for about 50 minutes.

Add the kidney and pinto beans and *masa harina*. Continue to simmer, uncovered, until the chili is slightly thickened, 5–7 minutes. Season to taste with salt and serve in large bowls.

Note: Ask the butcher to grind the meat fresh for chili, using the large holes of a meat grinder to give it a coarse texture.

Serving Tip: Accompany this chili with small bowls of sour cream, salsa, shredded Cheddar cheese, and chopped green (spring) onions.

MAKES 8–10 SERVINGS

MASA HARINA

There are as many versions of chili as there are chili cooks. This version uses a signature flavor of the American Southwest: *masa harina*. The Mexican corn flour used for making tortillas and tamales, *masa harina* is made by grinding corn kernels that have been simmered in a slaked lime solution and then dried. It is sold in well-stocked food stores and in Latin markets. A few tablespoons of *masa harina* added to the chili near the end of cooking both thickens the liquid slightly, giving it a welcome body, and imparts a subtle corn flavor.

---

5 tablespoons (2½ fl oz/75 ml) vegetable oil

3 lb (1.5 kg) beef chuck, ground (minced) for chili (see Note)

3 large yellow onions, finely chopped

8 cloves garlic, minced

1 jalapeño chile, seeded and finely chopped

½ cup (1½ oz/45 g) chili powder

2 tablespoons ground cumin

1 tablespoon ground oregano

2 teaspoons ground coriander

1½ cups (12 fl oz/375 ml) lager-style beer

2½ cups (20 fl oz/625 ml) beef stock (page 110) or prepared broth

1 can (28 oz/875 g) crushed tomatoes

1 can (15 oz/470 g) kidney beans, rinsed and drained

1 can (15 oz/470 g) pinto beans, rinsed and drained

3 tablespoons *masa harina (far left)*

Salt

SHRIMP BISQUE

3 tablespoons unsalted butter

1 yellow onion, thinly sliced

1 carrot, peeled and thinly sliced

2 cloves garlic, thinly sliced

2 lb (1 kg) raw shrimp (prawns), shelled and deveined (page 115), shells reserved

4 plum (Roma) tomatoes, about ¾ lb (375 g) total weight, coarsely chopped

4 cups (32 fl oz/1 l) fish stock or chicken stock (pages 110–11), prepared broth, or water

½ cup (1 oz/30 g) fine fresh bread crumbs

½ cup (4 fl oz/125 ml) heavy (double) cream

2 tablespoons dry sherry

Salt

Pinch of cayenne pepper

2 tablespoons finely chopped fresh flat-leaf (Italian) parsley

In a large saucepan over medium heat, melt the butter. Add the onion, carrot, and garlic and sauté until slightly softened, about 2 minutes. Add the shrimp shells and continue to sauté until the shells are bright pink and the vegetables softened, about 5 more minutes. Add the tomatoes and the stock and cook until the tomatoes are softened and the stock is aromatic, about 5 minutes longer. Remove the shrimp shells and discard.

In a blender or food processor, process the mixture in batches until finely chopped. Pass the finely chopped mixture through a fine-mesh sieve or food mill set over a soup pot, pressing on the solids with the back of a spoon. Discard the solids in the sieve.

Reserve about 24 shrimp to finish the soup and add the remaining shrimp and the bread crumbs to the pot. Cook over medium heat until the shrimp turn pink and are opaque throughout and the bread crumbs have been absorbed, about 3 minutes. Remove from the heat. In the blender or food processor, purée the soup in batches until smooth. Alternatively, process with a handheld blender in the pot until smooth.

Return the purée to medium heat and add the cream, sherry, salt to taste, and the cayenne pepper. Cook for another 2 minutes to blend the flavors. Taste and adjust the seasoning.

Cut the reserved shrimp into 1-inch (2.5-cm) pieces. Just before serving, add the shrimp pieces to the soup and cook until they turn pink and are opaque throughout, 1–2 minutes longer.

Ladle the soup into warmed bowls and garnish with the parsley. Serve immediately.

MAKES 6–8 SERVINGS

ABOUT BISQUE

The term *bisque* refers to a particular type of soup: a puréed seafood soup made with cream. Shrimp or lobster is the typical star of a bisque. The meaning of the term has broadened in recent years to include creamy puréed vegetable soups as well.

SIMPLE SOUPS

Sometimes a simple meal is in order—just an uncomplicated bowl of soup, perhaps with a crusty loaf. Every recipe that follows here meets that profile. All are recipes that go together quickly with little fuss. Many are also vegetarian, or can easily be made so by choosing a vegetable stock over a meat one. Every one, however, offers delicious fare that, with only a minimum amount of time in the kitchen, can turn into a satisfying meal.

POTATO-LEEK SOUP
WITH FENNEL AND WATERCRESS

In a soup pot over medium heat, warm the oil. Add the leeks and sauté, stirring occasionally, until soft, 4–5 minutes. Add the fennel and potatoes and continue to sauté, stirring occasionally, until slightly softened, about 10 minutes longer.

Add the stock and bring to a simmer. Partially cover and cook until the vegetables are completely softened, about 20 minutes. Add the watercress and cook until the watercress is wilted but is still bright green, 2 minutes longer. Remove from the heat.

In a blender or food processor, purée the soup in batches until smooth and return the soup to the pot. Alternatively, process with a handheld blender in the pot until smooth. Season to taste with salt and white pepper. Return the soup to medium heat and reheat gently.

Ladle the soup into warmed bowls and garnish with fennel leaves. Serve immediately.

MAKES 6–8 SERVINGS

FENNEL
Similar in appearance to celery, with a large bulb on the end, fennel has a faint licorice flavor. It is available year-round but is at its peak from October to March. Select creamy-colored bulbs with no browning, topped by crisp stems and feathery green leaves. Cut the stems off about 2 inches (5 cm) from the bulb and use only the bulb, trimming away the base of the core if it is thick and tough. The leaves make an excellent garnish and also can be used for flavoring soups and salads.

3 tablespoons olive oil

2 leeks, including tender green parts, coarsely chopped

2 fennel bulbs, about 1 lb (500 g) total weight, thinly sliced *(far left)*, leaves reserved for garnish

2 baking potatoes, about 1 lb (500 g) total weight, peeled and coarsely chopped

6 cups (48 fl oz/1.5 l) chicken or vegetable stock (pages 110–11) or prepared broth

1 bunch watercress, stems removed

Salt and freshly ground white pepper

CARROT SOUP
WITH ORANGE AND GINGER

3 tablespoons olive oil

2 leeks, including tender green parts, thinly sliced

6 carrots, about 1 lb (500 g) total weight, peeled and thinly sliced

1 red potato, about ½ lb (250 g), peeled and coarsely diced

1½ teaspoons peeled and minced or grated fresh ginger

5 cups (40 fl oz/1.25 l) chicken or vegetable stock (pages 110–11) or prepared broth

½ cup (4 fl oz/125 ml) fresh orange juice

2 teaspoons grated orange zest

Salt and freshly ground white pepper

Thin orange slices for garnish (optional)

Fresh mint sprigs for garnish (optional)

In a saucepan over medium heat, warm the oil. Add the leeks and sauté until just slightly softened, about 3 minutes. Add the carrots, potato, and ginger and sauté until the vegetables are just softened, about 5 minutes longer.

Add the stock, cover partially, and simmer until the vegetables are completely softened, about 20 minutes. Remove from the heat.

In a blender or food processor, purée the soup in batches, leaving some texture, and return the soup to the pan. Alternatively, process with a handheld blender in the pan until the desired consistency is reached. Return the soup to medium heat and stir in the orange juice and zest. Season to taste with salt and white pepper.

Ladle the soup into warmed bowls and garnish each serving with an orange slice and a sprig of mint.

Serving Tip: For an alternative fried ginger garnish, peel a 5-inch (13-cm) piece of ginger and slice it into a very fine julienne. In a small frying pan over medium-high heat, pour vegetable oil to a depth of about ½ inch (12 mm). When the oil is hot, fry the julienned ginger until crisp and golden brown, 20–30 seconds. Use a skimmer to remove the ginger and transfer to a paper towel–lined plate or tray. When cool, divide the ginger into 4–6 portions and use to garnish each serving of soup.

MAKES 4–6 SERVINGS

GINGER

Pale brown, knobby fresh ginger adds a note of exotic, sweet spiciness to soups and other dishes. Look for smooth, shiny ginger with no cracks in the skin. Using a sharp knife or a vegetable peeler, remove the thin skin before slicing, chopping, mincing, or grating. To grate fresh ginger, use the finest rasps on a standard handheld grater or use a specially designed ginger grater, a small, flat ceramic or light metal tool with tiny, very sharp teeth.

CAULIFLOWER AND CHEESE SOUP

In a soup pot over medium-high heat, warm the oil. Add the onion and sauté until softened and very lightly colored, about 5 minutes. Add the garlic and caraway seeds and sauté for 1 minute. Do not let the garlic burn.

Add the cauliflower and stock and bring to a simmer. Reduce the heat to medium and cook until the cauliflower is softened, 20–25 minutes. Remove from the heat.

In a blender or food processor, purée the soup in batches until the cauliflower is smooth and the soup has a creamy consistency, then return the soup to the pot. Alternatively, process with a handheld blender in the pot until the desired consistency is reached. Whisk in the Cheddar cheese to completely incorporate. Season to taste with salt and white pepper.

Return the soup to medium heat and cook until heated through, about 2 minutes. To serve, ladle the soup into warmed bowls and sprinkle with the blue cheese and a pinch of parsley. Serve immediately.

MAKES 4–6 SERVINGS

PREPARING CAULIFLOWER

Cauliflower has a delicious, mild flavor that marries nicely with cheese and makes a wonderful soup. Select firm, tight cauliflower heads free of brown spots, avoiding those with loosely packed florets. Remove any green leaves from the head and, using a small, sharp knife, separate the head into florets. Cut away any tough, hard stem ends and discolored areas and discard. Leave any tender stems attached to the florets.

2 tablespoons olive oil

1 yellow onion, sliced

3 cloves garlic, minced

½ teaspoon caraway seeds

2 lb (1 kg) cauliflower, stemmed and cut into florets *(far left)*

4 cups (32 fl oz/1 l) vegetable stock (page 111) or prepared broth

1 cup (4 oz/125 g) shredded sharp Cheddar cheese

Salt and freshly ground white pepper

¼ cup (1 oz/30 g) crumbled blue cheese

1 tablespoon finely chopped fresh flat-leaf (Italian) parsley

PURÉE OF VEGETABLE SOUP

2 tablespoons olive oil

3 leeks, including light green parts, finely chopped

4 carrots, peeled and sliced

4 zucchini (courgettes), sliced

3 waxy or all-purpose potatoes *(far right)*, about 1 lb (500 g) total weight, peeled and thinly sliced

1½ tablespoons tomato paste

6 cups (48 fl oz/1.5 l) chicken stock (page 110) or prepared broth

1 cup (6 oz/185 g) canned chickpeas (garbanzo beans), rinsed and drained

1 tablespoon fresh lemon juice

Salt and freshly ground white pepper

3 tablespoons finely chopped fresh flat-leaf (Italian) parsley

1 tablespoon finely chopped lemon zest

In a large saucepan over medium heat, warm the oil. Add the leeks and sauté until softened, about 5 minutes. Add the carrots, zucchini, and potatoes and sauté until they begin to soften, about 3 minutes.

Add the tomato paste and stock, cover partially, and simmer until the vegetables are tender, 25–30 minutes. Add the chickpeas and cook until heated through, about 3 minutes longer. Stir in the lemon juice and salt and white pepper to taste. Remove the soup from the heat.

In a blender or food processor, purée the soup in batches until smooth and return the soup to the pan. Alternatively, process with a handheld blender in the pan until smooth. Return the soup to medium heat and reheat gently. Stir in 2 tablespoons of the parsley. Taste and adjust the seasoning.

Ladle the soup into warmed shallow bowls and garnish with the remaining 1 tablespoon parsley and the lemon zest. Serve immediately.

Serving Tip: To dress up this soup, consider adding a dollop of Basil Pesto (page 105) or Sun-Dried Tomato Pesto (page 56) as an additional garnish. Cheese Croûtes (page 112) would also be a good accompaniment.

MAKES 4–6 SERVINGS

POTATO VARIETIES

There are three basic types of potato: starchy, waxy, and all-purpose. Starchy potatoes are best for baking, while waxy and all-purpose will work well for this soup. Waxy potatoes, such as fingerlings, are low in starch and hold their shape when cooked, while all-purpose potatoes, including rose fir, Yukon gold, Yellow Finn, and white rose, are considered medium starch and can do double duty, in the oven and on the stove top. The white rose potato is especially good for its creamy consistency.

BROCCOLI-LEEK SOUP

In a large saucepan over medium heat, warm the oil. Add the leeks and sauté until softened, 3–5 minutes. Add the broccoli and continue to sauté, stirring frequently until slightly softened, about 2 minutes longer.

Add the stock and bring to a simmer over medium heat. Cover partially and cook until the vegetables are tender when pierced with a sharp knife, 15–20 minutes. Remove from the heat.

In a blender or food processor, purée the soup in batches until smooth and return the soup to the pan. Alternatively, process with a handheld blender in the pan until smooth. Return the soup to medium heat and reheat gently. Season to taste with salt and white pepper.

Ladle the soup into warmed bowls and garnish with the sour cream, croutons, and chives. Serve immediately.

MAKES 4 SERVINGS

CLEANING LEEKS

Because they are grown in loose, sandy soil, leeks often have grit lodged between their tightly packed leaves. To clean a leek, trim off the roots and the tough, dark tops of the leaves. Peel away the outer layer from the stalk and discard. Halve or quarter the leek lengthwise. (If the leek will be served whole, leave the root end attached and cut only three-fourths of the way down from the green top.) Rinse well under cold running water, pulling the layers of leaves apart slightly to wash away all of the grit.

2 tablespoons olive oil

2 leeks, including tender green parts, finely chopped

1½ lb (750 g) broccoli, trimmed, florets and stalks cut into 1-inch (2.5-cm) pieces

4 cups (32 fl oz/1 l) chicken stock (page 110) or prepared broth

Salt and freshly ground white pepper

¼ cup (2 oz/60 g) sour cream or plain yogurt

Garlic Croutons for garnish (page 72)

2 tablespoons finely chopped fresh chives

GARLIC STRACCIATELLA

6 cups (48 fl oz/1.5 l) chicken stock (page 110) or prepared broth

30 cloves garlic, root ends trimmed

2 fresh thyme sprigs

¾ lb (375 g) spinach leaves, thick stems removed, cut lengthwise into narrow strips

1 small carrot, peeled and cut into thin julienne strips

3 tablespoons finely chopped fresh flat-leaf (Italian) parsley

2 tablespoons grated Parmesan cheese

2 eggs

Salt and freshly ground white pepper

In a saucepan over medium-high heat, combine the stock, garlic, and thyme and bring to a boil. Reduce the heat to medium, cover, and simmer until the garlic is very soft, about 20 minutes. Discard the thyme.

Remove from the heat. In a blender or food processor, purée the soup in batches until the garlic is smooth and return the soup to the pan. Alternatively, process in the pan with a handheld blender until the garlic is smooth.

Return the purée to medium heat and add the spinach, carrot, parsley, and Parmesan cheese. Simmer until the spinach is wilted but still bright green and the cheese is melted, about 2 minutes. Remove from the heat.

Lightly beat the eggs with a fork and slowly pour into the soup, stirring with the fork until threads of cooked egg form. Season to taste with salt and white pepper. Ladle the soup into warmed bowls and serve immediately.

Note: Stracciatella means "little rag," a playful description of the shreds of spinach and egg in this classic Italian soup. The traditional version is enlivened here with the addition of garlic.

MAKES 6–8 SERVINGS

GARLIC

Simmering whole garlic cloves in stock mellows their pungency; once puréed, they add an earthy, rich, slightly sweet flavor to this soup. Buy garlic from a market with good turnover and do not buy more than a couple of weeks' worth of garlic at a time to ensure freshness. Do not use garlic that has a green center or is starting to sprout, for it will taste bitter. Removing the root end of a garlic clove will also help avoid bitterness. White-skinned American garlic is more strongly flavored than purplish red Mexican or Italian varieties.

ZUCCHINI PURÉE
WITH OREGANO CREAM

In a large saucepan over medium heat, warm the oil. Add the onion and sauté, stirring occasionally, until well softened, about 5 minutes. Add the zucchini and season to taste with salt and pepper. Continue to sauté until the onion and zucchini are well browned, 5–7 minutes longer.

Add the stock and oregano and bring to a simmer. Cover and cook until the vegetables are tender, 15–20 minutes. Remove the soup from the heat.

Meanwhile, make the oregano cream. In a small bowl, stir together the sour cream, oregano, and salt and pepper to taste. Refrigerate until ready to serve.

In a blender or food processor, purée the soup in batches until smooth and return the soup to the pan. Alternatively, process in the pan with a handheld blender until smooth. Return the soup to medium heat and reheat gently. Taste and adjust the seasoning with salt and pepper.

Ladle the soup into warmed bowls and garnish each bowl with a dollop of oregano cream. Serve immediately.

MAKES 4–6 SERVINGS

OREGANO

An aromatic, pungent, and spicy herb, oregano is used as a seasoning for all kinds of savory dishes. It is especially compatible with tomatoes and vegetables such as the zucchini in this recipe. Sometimes called wild marjoram, oregano is in fact related to marjoram and other members of the mint family, but it has a stronger aroma and less sweet flavor. Both Mexican and more mild Mediterranean varieties of oregano are widely available. Look for fresh green bunches at well-stocked markets.

2 tablespoons olive oil

1 yellow onion, finely chopped

6 zucchini (courgettes), trimmed and thinly sliced

Salt and freshly ground pepper

4 cups (32 fl oz/1 l) chicken stock (page 110) or prepared broth

2 tablespoons finely chopped fresh oregano

FOR THE OREGANO CREAM:

½ cup (4 oz/125 g) sour cream or plain yogurt

1 teaspoon finely chopped fresh oregano

Salt and freshly ground pepper

DINNER PARTY SOUPS

An elegant dinner party calls for a special first-course soup, something a bit unusual that guests will remember. The following soups stand apart thanks to out-of-the-ordinary ingredients, an elegant presentation, or a touch of the exotic. Special does not mean difficult, however; all are relatively quick to prepare.

THREE-MUSHROOM SOUP
WITH SHERRY

Soak the dried mushrooms in 3 cups (24 fl oz/875 ml) boiling water for 30 minutes.

Drain the soaked mushrooms, reserving 2 cups (16 fl oz/500 ml) of the soaking liquid. Strain the liquid through a fine-mesh sieve lined with cheesecloth (muslin) or a coffee filter to remove any grit. Set the liquid and mushrooms aside.

In a saucepan over medium heat, warm the oil. Add the onion and sauté, stirring occasionally, until softened, 5–7 minutes. Add the fresh button and shiitake mushrooms and cook, stirring, until slightly softened, about 3 minutes. Sprinkle with the flour and salt and pepper to taste. Stir to coat the mushrooms and to cook the flour, about 1 minute. Add the stock and the reserved mushroom liquid. Add the reserved drained mushrooms and reduce the heat to medium-low. Simmer until all the mushrooms are completely softened, about 15 minutes. Remove from the heat.

In a blender or food processor, purée the soup in batches, making sure to leave a little texture, and return the soup to the pan. Alternatively, process with a handheld blender in the pan until the desired consistency is reached. Return the soup to medium heat. Add the half-and-half and sherry and cook until the flavors are blended, about 3 minutes. Season to taste with salt and pepper.

To serve, ladle the soup into warmed bowls and garnish with the parsley. Serve immediately.

MAKES 4–6 SERVINGS

1½ oz (45 g) dried mushrooms such as porcini or shiitakes

3 tablespoons olive oil

1 yellow onion, finely chopped

1 lb (500 g) fresh button mushrooms, thinly sliced

½ lb (250 g) fresh shiitake mushrooms, thinly sliced

3 tablespoons all-purpose (plain) flour

Salt and freshly ground pepper

4 cups (32 fl oz/1 l) beef, chicken, or vegetable stock (pages 110–11) or prepared broth

½ cup (4 fl oz/125 ml) half-and-half (half cream)

¼ cup (2 fl oz/60 ml) dry sherry *(far left)*

2 tablespoons finely chopped fresh flat-leaf (Italian) parsley, plus some whole leaves

CRAB AND ASPARAGUS SOUP

4 cups (32 fl oz/1 l)
chicken stock (page 110)
or prepared broth

1 teaspoon peeled and
minced fresh ginger

½ lb (250 g) asparagus
spears, trimmed and cut
on the diagonal into
1-inch (2.5-cm) pieces

1 egg, well beaten

1 tablespoon cornstarch
(cornflour) mixed with
2 tablespoons water

2 teaspoons dry sherry

1 teaspoon Asian
sesame oil

1 teaspoon soy sauce

1 cup (6 oz/185 g) cooked
crabmeat, picked over for
shell fragments

In a large saucepan over medium-high heat, combine the stock
and ginger and bring to a rolling boil. Add the asparagus, reduce
the heat to medium, cover, and simmer, until the asparagus is
cooked but crisp-tender, about 3 minutes.

Reduce the heat to medium-low. Stir 2 tablespoons of the hot
stock into the beaten egg. Slowly pour the egg mixture into the
stock, stirring constantly to form even threads of cooked egg.

Add the cornstarch mixture, sherry, sesame oil, and soy sauce.
Cook, stirring, until the soup thickens slightly, about 1 minute.

Stir in the crabmeat and cook just until it is warmed through,
2–3 minutes. Taste and adjust the seasoning as desired. Ladle the
soup into warmed bowls and serve immediately.

MAKES 4 SERVINGS

CRABMEAT

Freshly cooked crabmeat is
sold by weight at fish markets.
The meat is either lump
crabmeat, which consists of
large, snowy white pieces, or
flake crabmeat, which is a
mixture of white and
somewhat darker meat in
smaller pieces. Both are good
choices for this soup.
Vacuum-packed pasteurized
and frozen crabmeat are also
available, although these are
less desirable options. Avoid
imitation crabmeat, or *surimi*,
which is made from pollack
or other white-fleshed fish
that is shaped, cooked,
flavored, and colored to
resemble crab.

BUTTERNUT SQUASH
AND ROASTED GARLIC PURÉE

WINTER SQUASH
Butternut squash (above, lower right) is delicious in this recipe, but nearly any hard-shelled, firm-fleshed winter squash will do. Yellow-fleshed Hubbard, common acorn (above, left), or multi-hued turban squash (above, upper right) are all good choices. Using a good-sized knife, halve the squash lengthwise. Scoop out any seeds with a serrated spoon that will remove any fibers as well. Using a sharp swivel-type vegetable peeler or a small, sharp knife, peel away the tough skin.

Preheat the oven to 350°F (180°C). Cut the squash in half length-wise and remove the seeds and any fibers *(left)*. Carefully remove the peel and cut the flesh into slices 1 inch (2.5 cm) thick.

In a roasting pan, combine the squash and garlic cloves. Drizzle with 2 tablespoons of the oil and toss until well coated. Pour in the water. Roast, stirring occasionally, until the squash and garlic are soft and golden, 50–60 minutes. Add a bit more water if the squash begins to scorch. Remove from the oven and set aside to cool slightly.

While the squash and garlic cloves are roasting, in a heavy frying pan over medium heat, warm the remaining 2 tablespoons oil. Add the leeks and sauté until golden brown, 12–15 minutes. Set aside.

In a blender, in batches, combine the roasted squash, garlic, and leeks with 1 cup (8 fl oz / 250 ml) of the stock. Purée until very smooth, about 1 minute.

Transfer the squash purée to a large saucepan. Stir in the remaining 4 cups (32 fl oz / 1 l) stock and bring to a simmer over medium heat. Season to taste with salt and white pepper.

Ladle the soup into warmed bowls and garnish with the chives. Serve immediately.

MAKES 4–6 SERVINGS

1 large or 2 small butternut squash, about 4 lb (2 kg) total weight

20 cloves garlic

4 tablespoons (2 fl oz/60 ml) olive oil

¼ cup (2 fl oz/60 ml) water

2 leeks, including tender green parts, finely chopped

5 cups (40 fl oz/1.25 l) vegetable stock (page 111) or prepared broth

Salt and freshly ground white pepper

2 tablespoons finely chopped chives or fresh flat-leaf (Italian) parsley

MISO SOUP

To make the dashi, combine the *kombu* and cold water in a large saucepan. Bring to a gentle simmer over medium heat (do not boil, or the broth will become bitter). Remove from the heat, cover, and let stand for about 5 minutes. Strain the broth into a clean saucepan, discarding the *kombu*. Gently reheat the broth over medium heat just until it begins to simmer. Remove from the heat and add the bonito flakes. Once the flakes are submerged, let stand for about 30 seconds. Strain the dashi into another clean saucepan.

Place the dashi over medium-high heat and whisk in the miso paste. Add the ginger and bring to a simmer. Cover the pan, reduce the heat to low, and simmer for about 3 minutes. Discard the ginger. Add the mushrooms, tofu, and green onion and bring to a simmer. Cook until the tofu is heated through and the mushrooms are slightly softened, about 1 minute. Taste and adjust the seasoning as desired.

Ladle the soup into warmed bowls and serve immediately.

MAKES 4 SERVINGS

MISO

A staple of the Japanese kitchen, miso is a fermented paste of soybeans and grain. Among the most common types of miso are white or *shiro-miso,* red or *aka-miso,* and yellow or *shinshu-miso,* all of which differ in taste (sweeter or saltier) and texture (smoother or coarser) as well as color. Miso, like the *kombu* (kelp) and bonito flakes (a type of mackerel) needed for making dashi, or stock, can be found in Japanese markets and well-stocked food stores.

MUSSELS MARINIÈRE

In a large stockpot over medium-high heat, combine the wine, shallots, butter, 2 tablespoons of the parsley, bay leaf, and pepper to taste. Bring to a simmer and cook, uncovered, until the broth is aromatic, 4–5 minutes.

Add the mussels, discarding any that do not close to the touch. Cover the pot tightly and steam the mussels until they open, about 5 minutes, shaking the pot occasionally so they cook evenly. Discard any mussels that failed to open.

To serve, spoon the mussels into large warmed soup bowls, ladle some broth over them, and sprinkle with the remaining parsley. Serve immediately, with baguette slices for dipping in the broth.

Variation Tip: If you prefer a thicker broth, add 1 cup (2 oz/60 g) fine fresh bread crumbs when simmering the broth.

MAKES 2–4 SERVINGS

2 cups (16 fl oz/500 ml) dry white wine

6 shallots, minced

6 tablespoons (3 oz/90 g) unsalted butter

4 tablespoons (⅓ oz/10 g) finely chopped fresh flat-leaf (Italian) parsley

½ bay leaf

Freshly ground pepper

4 lb (2 kg) mussels, well scrubbed and debearded (far left)

Baguette slices, for serving

CLEANING MUSSELS

You can use black mussels or New Zealand green-lipped mussels for this favorite French recipe. When buying either type, select ones that have tightly closed shells that are not cracked or broken. If a mussel is open, tap it; it should close promptly. To clean mussels, scrub the shells well under cold running water. The beard, a fibrous tuft near the hinge, should not be removed until just before cooking. Grasp it close to the shell and pull on it with a firm tug. Today, with so many farm-raised mussels in the market, beards are less fully formed and easier to remove.

HOT-AND-SOUR SOUP

1 oz (30 g) dried Chinese
black mushrooms or dried
shiitake mushrooms

2 tablespoons plus
1 teaspoon white wine
vinegar

1 tablespoon plus
1 teaspoon soy sauce

½ teaspoon Asian
sesame oil

1¼ teaspoons Asian
chile oil

Freshly ground pepper

5 cups (40 fl oz/1.25 l)
chicken stock (page 110)
or prepared broth

½ cup (2½ oz/75 g)
canned thinly sliced
bamboo shoots, rinsed
and drained

1 skinless, boneless whole
chicken breast, about ½ lb
(250 g), cut crosswise into
thin bite-sized slices

¼ lb (125 g) firm tofu,
drained and cut into
½-inch (12-mm) cubes

2 tablespoons cornstarch
(cornflour)

¼ cup (2 fl oz/60 ml) water

1 egg, well beaten

Soak the dried mushrooms in 3 cups (24 fl oz/750 ml) boiling water for 30 minutes. Drain the mushrooms and slice them thinly. Set aside.

In a small bowl, stir together the vinegar, soy sauce, sesame oil, chile oil, and ½ teaspoon pepper. Set aside.

In a saucepan over medium-high heat, bring the stock to a simmer. Add the drained mushrooms and bamboo shoots and cook until the stock is aromatic, about 3 minutes.

Reduce the heat to medium and add the chicken slices and tofu. Cook until the chicken is just opaque throughout and the tofu is heated through, about 2 minutes. Add the reserved vinegar-soy mixture and bring to a simmer.

In a small bowl, combine the cornstarch and water and stir until the cornstarch is dissolved. Add to the soup and stir until the soup begins to thicken.

Remove from the heat. Add the beaten egg, whisking with a fork until little shreds of cooked egg form. Taste and adjust the seasoning with vinegar, pepper, or soy sauce.

Ladle the soup into warmed bowls and serve immediately.

Serving Tip: Try serving this with a shredded cabbage salad dressed with rice wine vinegar, sugar, and a little oil.

MAKES 4 SERVINGS

REHYDRATING MUSHROOMS

To rehydrate dried whole mushrooms, place them in a bowl with boiling water to cover and let soak for 30 minutes, until soft. (If you are soaking dried mushroom slices, you can reduce the soaking time to 15–20 minutes.) Drain well. For extra mushroom flavor, reserve the soaking liquid and add it to the dish. Before using, strain the liquid through a sieve lined with cheesecloth (muslin) or a coffee filter to remove any grit.

ROASTED-VEGETABLE SOUP WITH SUN-DRIED TOMATO PESTO

SUN-DRIED TOMATO PESTO

In a food processor, with the motor running, add 1 clove garlic and process until minced. Turn off and add ½ cup (2½ oz/75 g) drained oil-packed sun-dried tomatoes, coarsely chopped; 2 tablespoons olive oil; 2 tablespoons finely chopped fresh basil; 2 tablespoons pine nuts; and salt and pepper to taste. Process until a thick paste forms, adding more oil as needed. Refrigerate in a covered container for up to 2 weeks. Makes about ½ cup (4 fl oz/125 ml).

Preheat the oven to 425°F (220°C). In a large, heavy roasting pan, combine the leeks, carrots, zucchini, eggplants, tomatoes, and potatoes. Add ½ cup (4 fl oz/125 ml) of the stock, the oil, and salt and pepper to taste and mix until the vegetables are well coated. Roast until the vegetables are softened, turning once to make sure they do not burn, about 40 minutes total.

In a blender, in batches, combine the vegetables with ½ cup (4 fl oz/125 ml) of the stock and purée until smooth. Transfer to a large saucepan over low heat, and stir in the remaining 3½ cups (28 fl oz/875 ml) stock, the basil, and the lemon juice. If needed, add a bit more stock for the desired consistency. Cook for 3 minutes to allow the flavors to blend. Season to taste with salt and pepper.

Ladle the soup into warmed bowls and add 1 tablespoon of the pesto to each bowl. Serve immediately.

Note: This soup requires the use of a blender for puréeing, as a food processor or handheld blender will not fully break down the fibers in some of these vegetables.

MAKES 4–6 SERVINGS

2 leeks, including tender green parts, finely chopped

4 carrots, peeled and cut into 2-inch (5-cm) pieces

2 zucchini (courgettes), cut into 2-inch (5-cm) pieces

2 Asian eggplants (slender aubergines), cut into 2-inch (5-cm) pieces

2 large tomatoes, quartered

2 white rose or other all-purpose potatoes (page 35), about 10 oz (315 g) total weight, peeled and cut into 2-inch (5-cm) pieces

4½ cups (36 fl oz/1.1 l) chicken stock (page 110) or prepared broth, or as needed

2 tablespoons olive oil

Salt and freshly ground pepper

2 tablespoons finely chopped fresh basil

2 tablespoons fresh lemon juice

4–6 tablespoons (2–3 fl oz/ 60–90 ml) Sun-Dried Tomato Pesto *(far left)*

SUMMER SOUPS

Soup makers welcome the warm weeks of summer for two reasons. First, a wealth of sun-ripened seasonal ingredients—tomatoes, corn, cucumbers, squash, peppers (capsicums)—greets them at grocery stores, at farmers' markets, and in their backyard gardens. Second is the opportunity to serve cold soups, the perfect antidote to soaring temperatures.

RED PEPPER AND TOMATO SOUP

In a large nonaluminum saucepan over medium heat, warm the olive oil. Add the onion and sauté until softened, 3–4 minutes.

Reduce the heat to medium-low and add the tomatoes, bell peppers, garlic, chile, and stock. Cover partially and cook until the vegetables are softened, about 20 minutes. Remove from the heat.

In a blender or food processor, purée the vegetables in batches until smooth. Alternatively, process with a handheld blender in the pan until smooth. Pass the puréed soup through a medium-mesh sieve set over a serving bowl, pressing on the pulp. Discard any solids left in the sieve. Season to taste with salt and pepper. Taste and adjust the seasoning. Let cool to room temperature and then cover and refrigerate the soup until it is well chilled, for at least 4 hours.

Taste and adjust the seasoning again just before serving. Ladle the soup into chilled bowls and garnish with a dollop of sour cream and a sprinkling of parsley. Serve immediately.

MAKES 4–6 SERVINGS

CHIPOTLE CHILES

The chipotle chile, which is actually a dried and smoked jalapeño, adds a smoky, spicy, surprisingly sweet flavor to any dish in which it is used. It varies in color from dark tan to chestnut brown. While chipotles may be found packed dry in plastic, look for canned chipotles in adobo sauce, a mixture of vinegar, tomatoes, and herbs. A splash of the sauce can be added along with the chile to flavor and add heat to this soup. Chipotles in adobo are available in the ethnic food aisle of most supermarkets.

3 tablespoons olive oil

1 yellow onion, chopped

6 large tomatoes, about 3 lb (1.5 kg) total weight, coarsely chopped

4 large red bell peppers (capsicums), coarsely chopped

3 cloves garlic, thinly sliced

½ chipotle chile in adobo *(far left)*

2 cups (16 fl oz/500 ml) chicken or vegetable stock (pages 110–11) or prepared broth

Salt and freshly ground pepper

¼ cup (2 oz/60 g) sour cream or plain yogurt

2 tablespoons chopped fresh flat-leaf (Italian) parsley

HERBED CUCUMBER SOUP WITH TOASTED ALMONDS

½ cup (2½ oz/75 g) plus 2 tablespoons coarsely chopped blanched almonds (see Note)

1 English (hothouse) cucumber, halved and seeded if necessary *(far right)*

1½ cups (12 oz/375 g) low-fat plain yogurt

1½ cups (12 fl oz/375 ml) buttermilk

¼ cup (⅓ oz/10 g) finely chopped fresh flat-leaf (Italian) parsley

1 clove garlic, minced

2 tablespoons finely chopped fresh chives

3 tablespoons finely chopped fresh dill

Salt and freshly ground white pepper

Preheat the oven to 350°F (180°C). Spread the almonds on a baking sheet and toast until lightly browned and aromatic, 5–7 minutes. (The almonds will continue to toast after you remove them from the oven, so cook them just a shade lighter than desired. They will become darker and crisper as they cool.) Let cool and set aside.

Coarsely chop half of the cucumber. In a food processor, purée it for about 20 seconds.

In a bowl, combine the yogurt and buttermilk. Stir in the puréed cucumber, parsley, garlic, chives, 2 tablespoons of the dill, and ½ cup of the almonds until well combined.

Chop the remaining cucumber half into small dice and add it to the soup. Season to taste with salt and white pepper. Cover and refrigerate until well chilled, at least 4 hours.

Taste and adjust the seasoning again just before serving. Ladle into chilled bowls and garnish with the remaining 2 tablespoons toasted almonds and the remaining 1 tablespoon chopped dill. Serve immediately.

Note: Try to find blanched whole or halved almonds. Toasting the nuts brings out their inherently rich flavor and adds an interesting depth of taste to this refreshing soup.

MAKES 4–6 SERVINGS

ENGLISH CUCUMBERS

Also called hothouse or hydroponic cucumbers, English cucumbers are the best choice for this soup. These cucumbers have far fewer and softer seeds than other slicing cucumbers, and their seeds and skin are usually not bitter. They do not need to be peeled and may not need seeding at all.

CURRIED CORN SOUP

CURRY POWDER

A mixture of as many as twenty different spices, seeds, and herbs, curry powder exists in countless variations. In India, many cooks make it fresh daily or buy only a very small quantity at a time from a trusted purveyor. Large-scale commercial curry powders, while not as interesting as a personal blend, work fine for this recipe. Sample a few different brands to find one you like. Curry powder loses its flavor relatively quickly, so buy small amounts and discard any that sit on the shelf for longer than six months.

In large saucepan over medium heat, warm the oil. Add the leeks and sauté, stirring frequently, until softened, about 5 minutes. Add the potatoes and all but ½ cup (3 oz/90 g) of the corn kernels and continue to cook for about 2 minutes longer. Add the curry powder and cook for about 1 minute longer.

Add the stock and lemon juice and bring to a boil. Reduce the heat to medium-low, cover partially, and simmer until the potatoes are soft, about 20 minutes. Remove from the heat.

In a blender or a food processor, purée the soup in batches until smooth. Alternatively, process with a handheld blender in the pan until smooth. Pass the purée through a fine-mesh sieve or a food mill set over a serving bowl, pressing on the pulp. Discard any solids left in the sieve. Season to taste with salt and white pepper. Let cool to room temperature and then cover and refrigerate until well chilled, at least 4 hours.

Just before serving, bring a small saucepan three-fourths full of water to a boil. Add the reserved ½ cup corn kernels and blanch for 1 minute. Drain and let cool.

Ladle the soup into chilled bowls or mugs and garnish with the lemon slices, sour cream, corn kernels, and parsley.

MAKES 6 SERVINGS

2 tablespoons olive oil

2 leeks, including tender green parts, finely chopped

2 small red potatoes, about ½ lb (250 g) total weight, peeled and coarsely chopped

5 cups (30 oz/940 g) corn kernels (from about 6 large ears of corn)

2 teaspoons curry powder

6 cups (48 fl oz/1.5 l) chicken stock (page 110) or prepared broth

2 tablespoons fresh lemon juice

Salt and freshly ground white pepper

6 thin lemon slices

½ cup (4 oz/125 g) sour cream

3 tablespoons finely chopped fresh flat-leaf (Italian) parsley

TWO-PEA SOUP WITH FRESH MINT

2 tablespoons vegetable oil

6 green (spring) onions, white part only, finely chopped

1 head butter (Boston) lettuce, cored and shredded

3 tablespoons coarsely chopped fresh mint

4 cups (32 fl oz/1 l) chicken stock (page 110) or prepared broth

½ lb (250 g) sugar snap peas, trimmed and tough strings removed

1 cup (5 oz/155 g) shelled English peas (about 1 lb/500 g unshelled) or thawed frozen petite peas

1 tablespoon fresh lemon juice

Salt and freshly ground white pepper

FOR THE GARNISH:

¼ cup (2 oz/60 g) sour cream

1 tablespoon finely chopped fresh mint

1 tablespoon finely chopped green (spring) onion, tender green part only

In a large saucepan over medium heat, warm the oil. Add the green onions and sauté, stirring occasionally, until softened, 3–5 minutes. Add the shredded lettuce and sauté until wilted, about 5 minutes. Add the coarsely chopped mint, stock, all but 4 of the sugar snap peas, and the English peas; cover and simmer for 20 minutes. (If using thawed frozen peas, add them during the last 5 minutes.) Remove from the heat.

Thinly slice the 4 reserved sugar snap peas and set them aside.

In a blender, purée the soup in batches until smooth. Return the puréed soup to the pan and add the sliced sugar snap peas and lemon juice. Season to taste with salt and white pepper. Return the pan to medium heat, bring to a simmer, and cook for about 3 minutes to blend the flavors.

Remove the soup from the heat and pour into a serving bowl. Let cool to room temperature and then cover and refrigerate until well chilled, at least 4 hours.

Taste and adjust the seasoning again just before serving. Ladle the soup into chilled bowls and garnish with sour cream, finely chopped mint, and green onion.

Note: This soup requires the use of a blender for puréeing, as a food processor or handheld blender will not fully break down the fibers naturally present in sugar snap peas.

Serving Tip: On a cool night, this soup is excellent served warm. Be sure to reheat gently.

MAKES 4–6 SERVINGS

MINT VARIETIES

Fresh mint is a delicious complement to peas. Many mint varieties exist, most of them named for the distinctive flavor each carries along with its basic mint taste: lemon, pineapple, orange, spearmint, and even chocolate. A simple hearty mint, such as spearmint, is best in this recipe. Mint can flourish on a windowsill, so plant a pot or two near your kitchen, and you'll be rewarded with a steady supply. It may also be grown in the garden—but be warned that it grows easily and may take over!

SUMMER SQUASH
AND BUTTERMILK BISQUE

In a large soup pot over medium heat, warm the oil. Add the leeks and sauté until softened, 5–7 minutes. Add the squash and sauté until lightly browned, 5 minutes. Add the garlic and cook for 1 minute longer.

Add the stock, cover, and cook until the squash slices are tender, about 15 minutes. Remove from the heat.

In a blender or food processor, purée the soup in batches until smooth. Alternatively, process with a handheld blender in the pot until smooth. Transfer the puréed soup to a serving bowl. Let cool to room temperature and then cover and refrigerate until well chilled, at least 4 hours.

Just before serving, stir in the the buttermilk, 2 tablespoons of the basil, the chives, and lemon juice. Season to taste with salt and pepper. Ladle the soup into chilled bowls and garnish with the remaining 2 tablespoons basil.

MAKES 6 SERVINGS

SUMMER SQUASH

Narrow, bright yellow summer squash are sunnier-colored cousins of the better-known green zucchini (courgette). Look for medium-sized squash, as large ones are often bitter and can be quite watery. You can also use other summer squash, such as the equally bright yellow crookneck, the green zucchini, or the scallop-edged pattypan, which comes in pale green, white, or yellow. Or, try a combination of types.

3 tablespoons olive oil

2 leeks, including tender green parts, finely chopped

6 summer squash, trimmed and thinly sliced

2 cloves garlic, minced

4 cups (32 fl oz/1 l) chicken stock (page 110) or prepared broth

1 cup (8 fl oz/250 ml) buttermilk

4 tablespoons (½ oz/10 g) finely chopped fresh basil

2 tablespoons finely chopped fresh chives

1 tablespoon fresh lemon juice

Salt and freshly ground pepper

TOMATO AND CORN SOUP WITH FRESH BASIL

2 tablespoons olive oil

2 leeks, white part only, finely chopped

5 large tomatoes, about 2½ lb (1.25 kg) total weight, seeded (page 18) and coarsely chopped

2 tablespoons all-purpose (plain) flour

2½ cups (15 oz/470 g) corn kernels (from about 3 ears of corn), corn cobs reserved and cut in half

8 fresh basil leaves, plus sprigs for garnish

1 tablespoon plus 1 teaspoon tomato paste

3 cups (24 fl oz/750 ml) chicken stock (page 110) or prepared broth

Salt and freshly ground pepper

Garlic Croutons (page 72) or Cheese Croûtes (page 112) for garnish

¼ cup (2 oz/60 g) sour cream

In a large nonaluminum soup pot over medium heat, warm the oil. Add the leeks and sauté until softened, about 5 minutes. Add the tomatoes and cook until slightly softened, 3 minutes. Add the flour and cook, stirring constantly, for 2 minutes longer.

Add the corn kernels, corn cobs, basil leaves, tomato paste, and stock. Bring to a simmer over medium-low heat. Cover partially and simmer for about 25 minutes. Remove from the heat and discard the corn cobs.

In a blender or food processor, purée the soup in batches until smooth. Alternatively, process with a handheld blender in the pot until smooth. Pour the puréed soup through a fine-mesh sieve into a serving bowl. Season to taste with salt and pepper. Let cool to room temperature and then cover and refrigerate until well chilled, at least 4 hours.

Taste and adjust the seasoning just before serving. Ladle the soup into chilled bowls and top with a few croutons. Garnish each bowl with a spoonful of sour cream and a sprig of basil.

Notes: Sweet white corn is particularly delicious in this soup. To ensure a velvety texture, use a fine-mesh sieve when straining.

MAKES 4–6 SERVINGS

CORN OFF THE COB

To remove corn kernels from the cob, hold a husked ear upright in a bowl, stem end down. Using a sharp knife, carefully slice down between the kernels and the cob, allowing the kernels to fall in the bowl and rotating the cob slightly after each cut. (Some recipes call for the corn "milk" as well. Holding the cob over a bowl, run the back of the knife blade along the length of the corn to squeeze out every drop.) In this recipe, the stripped cobs are cut in half and added to the soup to add extra corn taste.

GAZPACHO

In a large nonaluminum bowl, combine the anchovy paste and tomato juice and whisk until the anchovy paste is dissolved. Add the tomatoes, stock, oil, vinegar, and garlic and whisk until blended. Season to taste with salt and pepper. Add the cucumbers, onion, and the ⅓ cup basil and mix well. Add the chopped red and yellow bell peppers, reserving 2 tablespoons for garnish.

In a blender, purée 3 cups (24 fl oz / 750 ml) of the soup. Return the purée to the large bowl. Cover and refrigerate until well chilled, at least 4 hours.

Just before serving, taste and adjust the seasoning with salt and pepper. Ladle the soup into chilled bowls and garnish with the reserved chopped bell peppers and the sour cream, croutons, and the remaining 2 tablespoons basil.

MAKES 6–8 SERVINGS

GARLIC CROUTONS

Remove the crusts from 4–6 slices coarse country bread, each ¾ inch (2 cm) thick. Cut the slices into ¾-inch (2-cm) cubes. In a frying pan over medium-high heat, combine ⅓ cup (3 fl oz/80 ml) extra-virgin olive oil and 4 cloves garlic, sliced lengthwise. Fry until the garlic turns brown, about 4 minutes. Do not allow it to burn. Using a slotted spoon, scoop out and discard the garlic. Add the bread cubes to the pan and fry, stirring often, until golden brown on all sides, about 5 minutes. Transfer to paper towels to drain.

2 teaspoons anchovy paste

4 cups (32 fl oz/1 l) tomato juice

3 lb (1.5 kg) ripe tomatoes, peeled and seeded (page 18), then finely chopped

2 cups (16 fl oz/500 ml) chicken or vegetable stock (pages 110–11) or prepared broth

2 tablespoons olive oil

2 tablespoons red wine vinegar

3 cloves garlic, minced

Salt and freshly ground pepper

3 cucumbers, peeled, seeded, and finely chopped

⅓ cup (1½ oz/45 g) finely chopped red onion

⅓ cup (½ oz/15 g) plus 2 tablespoons finely chopped fresh basil

1 red bell pepper (capsicum), finely chopped

1 yellow bell pepper (capsicum), finely chopped

½ cup (4 oz/125 g) sour cream

Garlic Croutons *(far left)* for garnish

PEACH AND YOGURT SOUP

2 lb (1 kg) ripe peaches,
peeled *(far right)*

1½ cups (12 oz/375 g)
peach yogurt

2 tablespoons tawny Port

⅓ cup (3 fl oz/80 ml)
Johannisberg Riesling

¼ teaspoon ground ginger

Pinch of ground nutmeg

Fresh mint leaves
for garnish

Cut the peeled peaches in half and remove the pits. Cut the peaches into small cubes. Cover and refrigerate ¼ cup (1½ oz/45 g) of the cubed peaches for garnish.

In a food processor, purée the remaining cubed peaches until they are smooth.

Pour the peach purée into a bowl and stir in the yogurt, Port, Riesling, ginger, and nutmeg. Whisk to blend well. Cover and refrigerate until well chilled, at least 4 hours.

Ladle the soup into chilled bowls and garnish with the reserved cubed peaches and mint leaves. Serve immediately.

Serving Tip: This soup is particularly good as a first course for a light outdoor luncheon. You could also serve it as a refreshing finale to a warm-weather dinner.

MAKES 4 SERVINGS

PEELING PEACHES

Any variety of peach or nectarine works for this soup. To peel fuzzy peaches with ease, blanch them first. Fill a large saucepan three-fourths full of water and bring it to a boil. Using a sharp knife, score an X in the blossom end of each peach. Immerse 2 or 3 peaches in the boiling water and leave for 15–30 seconds, just until the skin begins to wrinkle. Using tongs or a slotted spoon, transfer the peaches to a large bowl of ice water to cool completely, then peel away the skins. Repeat until all the peaches are peeled.

WINTER SOUPS

Winter is the season when cooks prepare big, hearty soups that draw more often from the kitchen shelf than from the produce stand. Bean and grain soups are particularly satisfying, as are a fragrant fish stew or Cajun-style gumbo.

TURKEY SOUP WITH BARLEY
AND MUSHROOMS
78

THREE-BEAN SOUP
81

SPICY SEAFOOD
AND SAUSAGE GUMBO
82

HEARTY BEET BORSCHT
WITH BEEF AND CABBAGE
85

BLACK BEAN SOUP
WITH SALSA CREAM
86

PROVENCE-STYLE FISH STEW
89

WHITE BEAN, PASTA,
AND SWISS CHARD SOUP
90

TURKEY SOUP WITH BARLEY AND MUSHROOMS

Soak the dried mushrooms in 2 cups (16 fl oz / 500 ml) boiling water for 30 minutes.

Drain the soaked mushrooms, reserving 1 cup (8 fl oz / 250 ml) of the soaking liquid. Strain the liquid through a fine-mesh sieve lined with cheesecloth (muslin) or a coffee filter to remove any grit. Using a kitchen towel, squeeze the mushrooms dry and cut into ¼-inch (6-mm) dice. Set aside the mushrooms and their soaking liquid.

In a large soup pot over medium-high heat, warm the oil. Add the leeks and sauté until nicely softened, 5–7 minutes. Stir in the fresh button and shiitake mushrooms, carrots, barley, and garlic. Sauté for 1 minute longer. Add the turkey and stock, reduce the heat to low, cover, and simmer until the barley is tender but not mushy, about 1½ hours.

Remove the turkey thighs from the pot. Discard the skin and cut the meat from the bones. Shred the meat into bite-sized pieces and return it to the pot. Add the reserved mushrooms and soaking liquid to the soup. Stir in the soy sauce and chopped parsley and simmer for 5 minutes longer. Season to taste with salt and pepper.

Ladle the soup into warmed bowls and serve immediately.

Make-Ahead Tip: This soup can be prepared up to 2 days ahead of serving, covered, and refrigerated. It can also be frozen for up to 2 months. When reheating, taste and adjust the seasoning with salt and pepper.

MAKES 8 SERVINGS

PEARL BARLEY

Barley, an ancient grain with a pleasant nutty flavor and chewy texture, is sold in three basic forms: hulled and left whole, sometimes referred to as whole-grain barley; flaked; and pearled. This last, which is known as pearl barley, has been hulled and the bran removed. It is then steamed and finally polished to a shape and sheen that recalls its namesake. Because it cooks more quickly than whole-grain barley, it is the type most commonly called for in recipes.

½ oz (15 g) mixed dried mushrooms

2 tablespoons olive oil

3 leeks, including tender green parts, coarsely chopped

½ lb (250 g) fresh white button mushrooms, coarsely chopped

¼ lb (125 g) fresh shiitake mushrooms, stemmed and coarsely chopped

2 carrots, peeled and coarsely chopped

½ cup (3½ oz / 105 g) pearl barley

3 large cloves garlic, minced

2 skinless turkey thighs, about 1½ lb (750 g) total weight

8 cups (64 fl oz / 2 l) chicken or beef stock (page 110) or prepared broth

2 teaspoons soy sauce

3 tablespoons finely chopped fresh flat-leaf (Italian) parsley

Salt and freshly ground pepper

THREE-BEAN SOUP

1 cup (7 oz/220 g) dried pinto beans

1 cup (7 oz/220 g) dried kidney beans

1 cup (7 oz/220 g) dried white beans

2 tablespoons olive oil

2 yellow onions, finely chopped

2 celery stalks, finely chopped

2 carrots, peeled and finely chopped

1 can (14½ oz/455 g) diced tomatoes, with juice

8 cups (64 fl oz/2 l) chicken stock (page 110) or prepared broth

2 cups (16 fl oz/500 ml) water

¼ cup (⅓ oz/10 g) finely chopped fresh flat-leaf (Italian) parsley

3 cloves garlic, minced

1 bay leaf

Salt and freshly ground pepper

Gremolata for garnish *(far right)*

Pick over the pinto, kidney, and white beans, discarding any stones or misshapen beans, and rinse well. In a large pot, combine the beans with cold water to cover by 3 inches (7.5 cm). Soak for at least 4 hours or up to overnight. Alternatively, for a quick-soak method, bring the beans and water to a rapid simmer (but not a boil), then simmer for 2 minutes. Remove from the heat, cover, and let stand for 1 hour. Drain the beans and set aside.

In a large soup pot over medium-high heat, warm the oil. Add the onions and sauté until slightly softened, about 3 minutes. Add the celery and carrots and continue to sauté until barely softened, about 3 minutes longer.

Add the drained beans, tomatoes and juice, stock, water, parsley, garlic, and bay leaf. Cover and bring to a boil. Reduce the heat to low and simmer until the beans are tender, about 1 hour. Remove from the heat and discard the bay leaf.

Transfer half of the soup to a blender or food processor and process until puréed. Return the puréed soup to the pot. Alternatively, using a handheld blender in the pot, process the soup until partially puréed, leaving some texture. Reheat gently over medium heat and season to taste with salt and pepper.

Ladle the soup into warmed bowls and garnish with the gremolata. Serve immediately.

Variation Tip: For a more refined soup texture, purée all the ingredients until completely smooth in a food processor or blender or in the pot with a handheld blender.

MAKES 8 SERVINGS

GREMOLATA

Traditionally used as a finishing touch for the Italian braised veal shanks known as osso buco, gremolata is an aromatic blend of lemon zest, garlic, and parsley that also complements the subtle bean flavors in this soup. To make the gremolata, in a small bowl, stir together 2 cloves garlic, minced; ¼ cup (⅓ oz/10 g) finely chopped fresh flat-leaf (Italian) parsley; and the finely chopped zest of 1 lemon.

SPICY SEAFOOD
AND SAUSAGE GUMBO

OKRA

Indispensable to a good gumbo, okra are slender, ridged green seedpods with pointed ends. During cooking, the cut pods release a slimy substance that thickens the gumbo. Sautéing the okra before adding it to the other ingredients turns it a lovely golden brown and lessens its viscous quality. A dash of filé powder (ground sassafras leaves), traditional in gumbo, also acts as a thickener and can be found in the spice aisle at many well-stocked markets.

Dice the onion and the bell peppers. Set aside. Trim the stems from the okra pods, then cut the pods crosswise into slices ½ inch (12 mm) thick. In a large, heavy soup pot over medium heat, warm 2 tablespoons of the oil. Add the okra and sauté, stirring occasionally, until golden brown and softened, about 15 minutes. Transfer to a bowl and set aside.

In the same pot over medium heat, warm the remaining 6 table-spoons oil for 2 minutes. Whisk in the flour until incorporated. Cook the mixture, or roux, stirring constantly with a wooden spoon, until dark brown, about 4 minutes. Do not let the roux turn black. Add the onion and bell peppers and cook, stirring occasionally, until softened, 8–10 minutes. Add the garlic and cook for 1 minute longer.

Add the reserved okra, tomatoes and juice, stock, bay leaves, Creole seasoning, and salt and pepper to taste. Bring to a boil over medium-high heat and then reduce the heat to medium-low and simmer for 30 minutes to blend the flavors.

Stir in the sausage, shrimp, and crabmeat and cook until the sausage is heated through and the shrimp are pink, 3 minutes longer. Sprinkle in the filé powder and stir for 30 seconds. Remove from the heat and discard the bay leaves.

To serve, spoon rice into warmed bowls, ladle the gumbo on top, and garnish with the parsley.

Serving Tip: Serve the gumbo with a scoop of white rice. Two cups (14 oz/440 g) uncooked rice will make enough for 6 servings. For extra heat and zest, pass hot-pepper sauce at the table.

MAKES 6 SERVINGS

1 large yellow onion

1 *each* red and green bell pepper (capsicum)

½ lb (250 g) okra

½ cup (4 fl oz/125 ml) canola or vegetable oil

6 tablespoons (2 oz/60 g) all-purpose (plain) flour

3 cloves garlic, minced

1 can (14½ oz/455 g) diced tomatoes, with juice

5 cups (40 fl oz/1.25 l) fish stock (page 111) or bottled clam juice

2 bay leaves

2½ tablespoons Creole seasoning blend

Salt and pepper

½ lb (250 g) andouille sausage, sliced into 1-inch (2.5-cm) pieces

1 lb (500 g) large shrimp (prawns), shelled and deveined (page 115)

1 cup (6 oz/185 g) crabmeat, picked over for shell fragments

1 teaspoon filé powder

2 tablespoons finely chopped fresh parsley

HEARTY BEET BORSCHT WITH BEEF AND CABBAGE

6 beets, trimmed *(far right)*

3 tablespoons olive oil

3 lb (1.5 kg) boneless stewing beef, cut into bite-sized pieces

2 leeks, including tender green parts, finely chopped

2 carrots, peeled and coarsely chopped

1 can (14½ oz/455 g) diced tomatoes, well drained

1 head green cabbage, coarsely shredded

2½ qt (2.5 l) water

2 tablespoons tomato paste

6 fresh dill sprigs, plus 2 tablespoons finely chopped

5 tablespoons (2½ fl oz/ 75 ml) red wine vinegar

⅓ cup (2½ oz/75 g) plus 1 tablespoon firmly packed brown sugar

Salt and freshly ground pepper

½ cup (4 oz/125 g) sour cream

In a large saucepan over medium heat, combine the beets with water to cover by 1 inch (2.5 cm). Simmer until fork-tender, 45–60 minutes. Transfer the beets to a colander, reserving 2 cups (16 fl oz/500 ml) of the cooking liquid. Rinse under cold running water, drain, and peel. Cut the beets into ¾-inch (2-cm) pieces and set aside.

In a large soup pot over medium-high heat, warm 2 tablespoons of the oil. Brown the beef in batches, 5–7 minutes for each batch. Transfer to a plate and set aside.

Add the remaining 1 tablespoon oil to the pot. Add the leeks and carrots and sauté until softened and lightly browned, 5–7 minutes.

Add the reserved beet-cooking liquid, beef, tomatoes, cabbage, water, tomato paste, and dill sprigs, stirring to scrape up the browned bits from the bottom of the pot. Bring to a simmer over medium heat, cover partially, and cook until the beef is tender when pierced with a fork, about 1½ hours.

Add the reserved beets, vinegar, brown sugar, and salt and pepper to taste and simmer for 5 minutes longer. Taste and adjust the seasoning. Remove and discard the dill sprigs.

To serve, ladle the borscht into warmed bowls and garnish with the sour cream and chopped dill.

Make-Ahead Tip: The flavor of this soup improves if the soup is made a day before serving and reheated. The extra time allows the flavors to mellow and deepen.

Serving Tip: Serve with hunks of warm bread and butter.

MAKES 8–10 SERVINGS

COOKING BEETS

To prepare the beets, trim off the beet greens but leave 1 inch (2.5 cm) of the stem and the root end (usually a wispy tail) intact. Scrub the beets well, being careful not to break the skin, then boil as directed. To avoid red hands and stained cutting boards when working with the cooked beets, don kitchen gloves and protect the cutting board with a piece of plastic wrap or waxed paper.

BLACK BEAN SOUP WITH SALSA CREAM

Pick over the beans, discarding any stones or misshapen beans, and rinse well. In a large pot, combine the beans with cold water to cover by 3 inches (7.5 cm). Soak for at least 4 hours or up to overnight. Alternatively, for a quick-soak method, bring the beans and water to a rapid simmer (but do not boil), then simmer for 2 minutes. Remove from the heat, cover, and let stand for 1 hour. Drain the beans and set aside.

In a large soup pot over medium heat, warm the oil. Add the onions and sauté until softened, about 3 minutes. Add chile to taste, garlic, bell pepper, cumin, coriander, and oregano. Sauté, stirring frequently, until the vegetables are softened and the mixture is very aromatic, 7–10 minutes.

Add the beans, water, and ham hock, cover partially, and simmer over medium heat until the beans are soft, 1–1½ hours. Remove from the heat and discard the ham hock.

In a blender or food processor, purée the soup in batches, leaving some texture, and return the soup to the pot. Alternatively, process with a handheld blender in the pot until the desired consistency is reached. Add the lime juice, minced cilantro, and salt and pepper to taste. If the soup is too thick, thin it with water. (If you prefer a velvety consistency, purée the soup until smooth, then pour it through a fine-mesh strainer into a saucepan.) Reheat gently over medium heat.

Just before serving, make the salsa cream. In a small bowl, stir together the sour cream, lime juice, salsa, and salt and pepper.

Ladle the soup into warmed bowls and garnish each bowl with the salsa cream and a cilantro sprig.

MAKES 6–8 SERVINGS

SEEDING CHILES

The compound responsible for a chile's "fire" is called capsaicin. Although capsaicin is largely concentrated in the chile's ribs, or inner white membranes, some of the heat is transferred to the attached seeds and flesh as well. To remove most of the ribs and seeds from a fresh chile, using a small, sharp knife, slit the chile lengthwise, cut around the stem end, and pull the stem away, removing the clinging seeds with it. Then, using the knife, scrape away any remaining seeds and ribs.

2 cups (14 oz / 440 g) dried black beans

2 tablespoons canola oil

2 yellow onions, finely chopped

1 or 2 jalapeño chiles, seeded and minced *(far left)*

3 cloves garlic, minced

1 small red bell pepper (capsicum), diced

1 teaspoon ground cumin

1 teaspoon dried coriander

1 teaspoon dried oregano

8 cups (64 fl oz / 2 l) water

½ small ham hock or ham bone

2 tablespoons fresh lime juice

2 tablespoons minced fresh cilantro (fresh coriander), plus 6–8 sprigs

Salt and pepper

FOR THE SALSA CREAM:

½ cup (4 oz / 125 g) sour cream

2 tablespoons fresh lime juice

2 tablespoons purchased fresh salsa

Salt and pepper to taste

PROVENCE-STYLE FISH STEW

2 tablespoons olive oil

2 yellow onions, finely chopped

2 carrots, peeled and finely chopped

1 small fennel bulb, thinly sliced

3 large cloves garlic, minced

3 anchovy fillets, well rinsed, drained, and finely chopped *(far right)*

1 can (28 oz/875 g) diced tomatoes, with juice

2 cups (16 fl oz/500 ml) full-bodied red wine such as Zinfandel or Merlot

2 cups (16 fl oz/500 ml) fish stock (page 111) or bottled clam juice

2 orange zest strips, 2 inches long by ½ inch wide (5 cm by 12 mm)

Pinch of saffron threads

2 lb (1 kg) firm white fish fillets such as cod, halibut, monkfish, or mahimahi, cut into bite-sized pieces

Salt and freshly ground pepper

¼ cup (⅓ oz/10 g) finely chopped fresh flat-leaf (Italian) parsley

In a large soup pot over medium-high heat, warm the oil. Add the onions and sauté, stirring occasionally, until softened and very lightly browned, 5–7 minutes. Add the carrots and fennel and continue to sauté until the vegetables are slightly softened, 4–5 minutes. Add the garlic and cook for 1 minute longer.

Add the anchovies, tomatoes and juice, wine, stock, and orange zest. Reduce the heat to medium and bring to a simmer. Cover partially and cook until the soup is highly aromatic and the vegetables are well softened, about 15 minutes.

Remove and discard the zest. In a food processor or blender, purée about one-third of the soup and return the puréed soup to the pot. Alternatively, process briefly in the pot with a handheld blender, leaving plenty of texture. Add the saffron and fish. Cook over medium heat until the fish is just opaque throughout, 8–10 minutes. Season to taste with salt and pepper.

Ladle the soup into warmed bowls. Garnish with the parsley. Serve immediately.

Serving Tip: Serve with slices from a loaf of fresh French bread for dipping in the broth.

MAKES 6 SERVINGS

ANCHOVIES

Either salt-packed or olive oil–packed anchovies may be used for this dish. Oil-packed anchovies, sold in jars or cans, are already filleted and need only to be rinsed. Salt-packed anchovies, a specialty of Italy, are not filleted and have a firmer texture. Scrape off their skins and remove any fins. Using the tip of a small knife, split the anchovies open and lift out their backbones. Rinse the anchovies well before using.

WHITE BEAN, PASTA, AND SWISS CHARD SOUP

SOAKING BEANS

To prepare dried beans for cooking, pick over the beans, discarding any stones or misshapen beans, and rinse well. Put the beans in a large bowl, add cold water to cover generously, and soak for at least 4 hours or up to overnight. Drain and proceed as directed. If short of time, use the quick-soak method: Combine the beans and water to cover by 3 inches (7.5 cm) and simmer vigorously for 2 minutes. Remove from the heat, cover, and let stand for 1 hour, then drain and proceed as directed.

Drain the beans. In a large soup pot over medium heat, warm the oil. Add the onions and sauté, stirring occasionally, until softened, about 5 minutes. Add the carrots and sauté for 3 minutes. Add half of the Swiss chard and sauté until wilted, about 3 minutes. Add the stock, beans, tomatoes, basil, and garlic and simmer, partially covered, until the beans are tender, about 1 hour. Remove from the heat.

Meanwhile, in a pot of salted boiling water, cook the pasta until al dente, 3–5 minutes, depending on its thickness. Drain in a colander and set aside.

In a blender or food processor, purée the soup in batches, leaving some texture, and return the soup to the pot. Alternatively, process in the pot with a handheld blender until the desired consistency is reached.

Return the puréed soup to medium-high heat and add the cooked pasta and the remaining chard. Cook until the chard is wilted but still retains some color, about 3 minutes. Add salt and pepper to taste and 2 tablespoons of the parsley. Taste and adjust the seasoning.

Ladle the soup into warmed bowls and garnish with the remaining 2 tablespoons parsley and the Parmesan cheese. Serve the soup immediately.

Make-Ahead Tip: You can make this soup up to 3 days before serving and refrigerate it, or you can freeze it for up to 2 months. In either case, do not add the pasta until you reheat the soup, as the soup will become too thick upon sitting. Remember to taste and adjust the seasoning when reheating.

MAKES 6 SERVINGS

1 cup (7 oz/220 g) dried Great Northern or cannellini beans, soaked *(far left)*

2 tablespoons olive oil

2 yellow onions, coarsely chopped

2 carrots, peeled, and coarsely chopped

1 small bunch red Swiss chard, thick stems removed, cut into thin julienne strips

6 cups (48 fl oz/1.5 l) chicken stock (page 110) or prepared broth

1 cup (6 oz/185 g) chopped canned tomatoes

3 tablespoons finely chopped fresh basil

3 cloves garlic, minced

Salt and freshly ground white pepper

¾ cup (2½ oz/75 g) fine egg noodles or broken capellini

4 tablespoons (⅓ oz/10 g) finely chopped fresh flat-leaf (Italian) parsley

6 tablespoons (1½ oz/45 g) grated Parmesan cheese

CHICKEN SOUPS

From the classic American chicken noodle soup (page 10) to the spicy Mexican version or the elegant Japanese one, every culture has its own take on chicken soup. The reason is not hard to see: the restorative properties of a hot bowl of chicken soup are well known. It can fight off the sniffles, battle the flu, or simply boost your spirits on a cold day or after a long week.

CHICKEN SOUP
WITH FLUFFY MATZO BALLS

MAKING SCHMALTZ

To make schmaltz, dice the skin and fat of one chicken into 1-inch (2.5-cm) pieces. Cook in a heavy frying pan over medium-low heat, turning occasionally, until the fat melts away from the crisp cracklings. Let the liquid fat cool slightly, then strain through a sieve lined with cheesecloth (muslin). You should have about ⅓ cup (3 fl oz/80 ml). Cover and refrigerate for up to 3 days, softening in a small saucepan over low heat before using. Schmaltz can also be found in well-stocked food stores and Jewish delis.

Cut the chicken into serving pieces, removing and reserving the skin and fat for making schmaltz *(left)*.

In a large soup pot, combine the chicken pieces, onions, carrots, celery, parsnip, and dill with water to cover (about 2½ qt/2½ l). Bring to a boil over medium-high heat. Reduce the heat to medium, cover partially, and simmer, periodically skimming and discarding the foam that rises to the surface, until the soup is full flavored, 1½–2 hours. Season to taste with salt. Stir in the parsley and cook for 1 minute longer.

Meanwhile, make the matzo balls. In a small bowl, whisk together the schmaltz and eggs. In a separate bowl, combine the matzo meal and salt. Add the schmaltz mixture to the matzo meal mixture and stir to mix well. Add the seltzer water and stir until blended. Cover the bowl and refrigerate for 20 minutes.

Bring a pot three-fourths full of water to a boil over medium-high heat. Reduce the heat to medium and drop rounded tablespoonfuls of matzo dough, about 1½ inches (4 cm) in diameter, into the barely simmering water. If you prefer, you can shape the balls with lightly oiled hands. Cover the pot and cook until the matzo balls are light and fluffy, 20–30 minutes.

Transfer the chicken pieces to a plate, let cool, and then shred the meat, discarding the bones. Return the shredded chicken meat to the soup.

To serve, place a matzo ball in each warmed bowl and then ladle in the soup. Serve immediately.

MAKES 6 SERVINGS

1 large fryer chicken,
3½–4 lb (1.75–2 kg)

2 yellow onions, finely
chopped

3 or 4 small, sweet carrots,
peeled and cut into
½-inch (12-mm) slices

2 celery stalks, cut into
½-inch (12-mm) slices

1 parsnip, peeled and cut
into ½-inch (12-mm) slices

Leaves from 1 bunch fresh
dill, coarsely chopped

Salt

3 tablespoons finely
chopped fresh flat-leaf
(Italian) parsley

FOR THE MATZO BALLS:

2 tablespoons schmaltz
(far left) or vegetable oil

2 eggs, lightly beaten

½ cup (2¼ oz/67 g)
matzo meal

1 teaspoon salt

2 tablespoons seltzer
water or any sparkling
water

TORTILLA SOUP
WITH CHICKEN AND AVOCADO

½ cup (4 fl oz/125 ml) plus 2 tablespoons vegetable oil

1 yellow onion, thinly sliced

2 cloves garlic

¼ cup (⅓ oz/10 g) plus 2 teaspoons chopped fresh cilantro (fresh coriander)

1 cup (6 oz/185 g) drained canned plum (Roma) tomatoes

½ teaspoon ground cumin

4 cups (32 fl oz/1 l) chicken stock (page 110) or prepared broth

1 skinless, boneless whole chicken breast, about ½ lb (250 g), cut into bite-sized strips

Salt and pepper

4 corn tortillas, preferably stale and dry

1 dried chile such as ancho, seeded

1 avocado, pitted, peeled, and diced

¼ cup (1 oz/30 g) shredded Monterey jack cheese

2 teaspoons fresh lime juice

In a frying pan over medium heat, warm 1 tablespoon of the oil. Add the onion, garlic, and the 2 teaspoons cilantro and sauté just until golden brown, about 10 minutes.

In a blender or food processor, combine the sautéed mixture and the tomatoes and process until smooth.

In the same frying pan over medium-high heat, warm another 1 tablespoon of the oil. Add the tomato mixture and cumin. Cook, stirring frequently, until thickened and darkened, 5–6 minutes.

Transfer the mixture to a large saucepan over medium-low heat and add the stock. Cover partially and simmer, stirring occasionally, until the soup is slightly thickened, about 20 minutes. Add the chicken strips and simmer until they are just opaque throughout, 2–3 minutes longer. Season to taste with salt and pepper.

While the soup is cooking, cut the tortillas in half and slice each half into thin strips. In a frying pan over medium-high heat, warm the ½ cup vegetable oil. Drop a tortilla strip in the oil, and if it sizzles immediately, the oil is ready. Drop handfuls of the tortilla strips into the oil and fry, turning with tongs, until crisp and browned, about 3 minutes. Using a slotted spoon, transfer to paper towels to drain.

In a small, dry frying pan over medium heat, toast the chile until fragrant, about 7 minutes. Shake the pan often; do not let the chile burn. Let cool, then crumble and set aside.

To serve, ladle the soup into warmed bowls. Divide the tortilla strips, crumbled chile, the ¼ cup cilantro, the avocado, cheese, and lime juice evenly among the bowls and serve immediately.

MAKES 4 SERVINGS

TOASTED TORTILLA STRIPS

If you would like to avoid extra fat, you can toast, rather than fry, the tortilla strips for this soup (and toast the chile simultaneously): Preheat the oven to 400°F (200°C). Spread the tortilla strips evenly on a baking sheet and bake until crisp and beginning to brown, 7–8 minutes. Remove from the oven and let cool. The chile in the recipe can be toasted alongside the tortilla strips in the oven, saving an extra step.

CHICKEN AND SOBA NOODLE SOUP

Bring a large saucepan of water to a boil over high heat. Add the noodles and cook until just tender, about 4 minutes. Drain and set aside.

In a large saucepan over medium-high heat, combine the stock, water, miso, and ginger. Whisk together and bring to a simmer, then reduce the heat to medium and simmer until the miso is completely dissolved, about 3 minutes.

Add the chicken strips and cook until the chicken is just opaque throughout, about 2 minutes. Add the spinach and cook until slightly softened but still bright green, about 1 minute. Add the green onions and cook for 1 minute longer. Taste and adjust the seasoning as desired.

Using tongs, divide the noodles evenly among warmed bowls and then ladle in the soup. Serve immediately.

Variation Tip: Turkey strips may be used in place of the chicken.

MAKES 4–6 SERVINGS

SOBA NOODLES

Thin, brownish gray soba noodles, made from buckwheat, are enormously popular in Japan, where they are prepared year-round. There, on hot summer days, the noodles are eaten cold, arranged on a bamboo lattice rack with dipping sauce, while on chilly winter days, the noodles are immersed in piping-hot broth. Soba noodles are available fresh and dried in Japanese markets; the dried variety may also be found in the ethnic aisle of well-stocked supermarkets. Look for yellow miso paste in the same places.

½ lb (250 g) dried soba noodles

4 cups (32 fl oz/1 l) chicken stock (page 110) or prepared broth

2 cups (16 fl oz/500 ml) water

¼ cup (2 oz/60 g) yellow miso (page 51)

1 teaspoon peeled and grated fresh ginger

1 skinless, boneless whole chicken breast, about ½ lb (250 g), cut into thin strips

2 cups (2 oz/60 g) packed baby spinach leaves

2 green (spring) onions, including tender green parts, thinly sliced

AVGOLEMONO

6 cups (48 fl oz/1.5 l) chicken stock (page 110) or prepared broth

½ cup (3½ oz/105 g) long-grain white rice

4 egg yolks, lightly beaten

¼ cup (2 fl oz/60 ml) fresh lemon juice

1 teaspoon finely chopped lemon zest

Salt and freshly ground white pepper

2 tablespoons finely chopped fresh flat-leaf (Italian) parsley

In a large saucepan over medium-high heat, bring the stock to a boil. Add the rice and cook, uncovered, until the rice is tender, about 15 minutes.

In a medium bowl, whisk together the egg yolks, lemon juice, and lemon zest.

Whisking constantly to prevent curdling, slowly pour 1 cup (8 fl oz/250 ml) of the hot stock into the egg mixture.

Reduce the heat under the stock to medium-low and slowly stir in the tempered egg mixture. Cook, stirring, until the soup is slightly thickened, 3–4 minutes. Do not let the soup boil. Season to taste with salt and white pepper.

Ladle the soup into warmed bowls and garnish with the parsley. Serve immediately.

MAKES 4 SERVINGS

TEMPERING EGGS

The success of this rich, lemony chicken-and-rice soup, a signature dish of Greece, depends on the proper tempering of the egg yolks before they are whisked into the soup, a step that helps to prevent curdling. Tempering is done by whisking a small amount of hot liquid into eggs, to heat them slightly before whisking them into a hot mixture. Once tempered eggs have been added to a hot mixture, do not allow the mixture to boil, which would also cause the eggs to curdle, rather than giving the soup a thick and creamy consistency.

THAI-STYLE CURRIED CHICKEN SOUP

In a soup pot over medium heat, warm the oil. Add the curry paste and cook, stirring, until fragrant, about 1 minute. Add the stock, coconut milk, lemongrass, ginger, chiles to taste, lime juice, and fish sauce and bring to a simmer. Stir well and simmer until fragrant, about 5 minutes.

Add the chicken strips and cook until just opaque throughout, about 2 minutes. Add the mushrooms and sliced basil and cook until the mushrooms are softened, 2 minutes longer.

Ladle the soup into warmed bowls and garnish with the whole basil leaves. Serve immediately

Note: Read the label on the coconut milk carefully to make sure it is unsweetened milk. Otherwise the soup will be cloyingly sweet.

MAKES 4–6 SERVINGS

LEMONGRASS

With its bulbous ivory-colored base and long, thin gray-green leaves, lemongrass resembles a green (spring) onion in shape and size. It imparts a lemony fragrance to many Southeast Asian dishes. Only the pale lower portion of lemongrass is used. Cut off and discard the fibrous tops and remove the tough outer leaves from the base. With the flat side of a broad knife blade or cleaver, crush the trimmed base and then cut as directed in a recipe. If it is used in large pieces, remove and discard them before serving.

1 tablespoon vegetable oil

1 tablespoon Thai red curry paste

3 cups (24 fl oz/750 ml) chicken stock (page 110) or prepared broth

3 cups (24 fl oz/750 ml) unsweetened coconut milk, well shaken (see Note)

1 large lemongrass stalk, trimmed and cut into 2-inch (5-cm) pieces *(far left)*

6 thin slices fresh ginger, unpeeled

2–4 Thai chiles, cut in half lengthwise

3 tablespoons fresh lime juice

2 tablespoons Asian fish sauce

¾ lb (375 g) skinless, boneless chicken breasts, cut into thin strips

½ lb (250 g) fresh white button mushrooms, thinly sliced

¼ cup (⅓ oz/10 g) thinly sliced fresh basil leaves, preferably Thai basil, plus small whole leaves for garnish

CHICKEN MINESTRONE WITH ORZO

3 qt (3 l) chicken stock (page 110) or prepared broth

2 skinless, boneless whole chicken breasts

4 carrots, peeled

2 large zucchini (courgettes)

½ lb (250 g) green beans

1 small Asian eggplant (slender aubergine)

2 yellow onions

2 tablespoons olive oil

½ small head green cabbage, shredded

¼ lb (125 g) fresh white button mushrooms, thinly sliced

3 cloves garlic, minced

2 tomatoes, peeled and seeded (page 18), then finely chopped

¼ cup (⅓ oz/10 g) finely chopped fresh basil

Piece of Parmesan cheese rind (see Note)

¼ cup (1¾ oz/55 g) orzo

1 can (15 oz/470 g) cannellini beans, rinsed and drained

Salt and pepper

½ cup (4 fl oz/125 ml) Basil Pesto *(far right)*

In a large saucepan over medium heat, bring 6 cups (48 fl oz/1.5 l) of the stock to a simmer. Add the chicken breasts and simmer until just tender and no trace of pink remains, 8–10 minutes. Remove from the heat and let the chicken cool in the liquid. Transfer the chicken to a cutting board and cut into 1-inch (2.5-cm) cubes. Set aside. Strain and reserve the stock.

Cut the carrots, zucchini, green beans, and eggplant into 1-inch (2.5-cm) pieces and finely chop the onions. In a large pot over medium heat, warm the oil. Add the onions and sauté, stirring occasionally, until slightly softened, 3–5 minutes. Add the carrots, zucchini, green beans, and eggplant and sauté them until they are slightly softened, about 3 minutes. Add the cabbage and sauté it just until it is softened, about 2 minutes. Add the mushrooms and sauté until softened, about 2 minutes. Add the garlic and sauté for 1 minute. Add the tomatoes, the reserved stock plus the remaining 6 cups stock, the basil, and the Parmesan rind. Raise the heat to medium-high and bring to a boil. Reduce the heat to medium and cook until the vegetables are tender, about 15 more minutes.

Add the orzo and cannellini beans and cook until the orzo is al dente, 8–10 minutes. Stir in the chicken and heat through. Remove and discard the Parmesan rind. Season to taste with salt and pepper.

Ladle the soup into warmed bowls and swirl a tablespoon of pesto into each bowl. Serve immediately.

Note: Adding the rind from a wedge of Parmesan cheese, preferably Parmigiano-Reggiano or grana cheese, to the simmering soup gives it a unique nutty, sweet flavor.

MAKES 8 SERVINGS

BASIL PESTO

In a food processor, combine 2 minced cloves garlic, 2 cups (2 oz/60 g) packed fresh basil leaves, and ½ cup (½ oz/15 g) fresh flat-leaf (Italian) parsley leaves. Process until finely chopped. Add 2 tablespoons pine nuts and process until finely chopped. With the motor running, slowly pour in ½ cup (4 fl oz/125 ml) olive oil. Process until thick. Add ¾ cup (3 oz/90 g) grated Parmesan cheese and pepper to taste and process to mix. Makes about 1½ cups (12 fl oz/375 ml).

SOUP BASICS

A simmering pot of soup signifies home cooking at its best. Few foods can boast the versatility of soup. Whether served as a first course at the beginning of an elegant dinner party, as a convenient meal in a bowl, or as a comforting restorative on a cold day, soup is both simple to prepare and satisfying.

TYPES OF SOUPS

Most soups can be divided into three basic categories: clear soups; puréed soups, often made with cream; and chunkier soups that blur the line between soups and stews, such as chili or gumbo.

PURÉEING

Partially or completely puréeing a soup can give it a robust texture or smooth consistency and is called for in many of the recipes in this book. Different ingredients provide soup with sufficient body to be puréed: root vegetables such as potatoes or carrots; squash; tomatoes; bread crumbs; or cooked grains such as rice or corn. Puréeing is easily accomplished with a food mill, food processor, or blender.

USING A FOOD MILL

A hand-cranked food mill purées soup by forcing ingredients through a perforated conical disk, which functions something like a sieve, removing fibers, skins, and seeds from vegetables like asparagus, corn, and tomatoes. Most mills come with both medium and fine disks, offering the cook a choice of coarser or smoother purées.

USING A FOOD PROCESSOR

A food processor purées soups almost instantaneously. First, fit the processor with the metal blade. Ladle a small batch of the cooked solids and a bit of the liquid into the food processor's bowl, being careful not to overfill. Close and pulse the machine several times, then process until the purée is the desired consistency. Take care to purée hot soups in small batches to avoid splattering.

When puréeing soup in a food processor, straining may be necessary to remove fibers, skins, or seeds. Remove them by pouring the purée into a sieve set over a large bowl. Using the back of a spoon, press the purée through the sieve, discarding any solids trapped in the wire mesh. Repeat in batches with the remaining purée. Stir to give the purée an even consistency, returning it to the pan if necessary for gentle reheating.

USING A STANDING BLENDER

Blenders make puréeing soups fast and easy. They can usually handle more liquid volume than food processors. They are sometimes more suitable than food processors for puréeing because they more fully break down the fibers naturally found in some vegetables. When using a blender, work in small batches, and start with the lowest speed. Gradually increase the speed until the desired consistency is reached.

USING A HANDHELD BLENDER

Handheld blenders, also called immersion blenders, have a blade that can be lowered directly into a pot of soup, blending large amounts of soup at a time with little mess. They also tend to incorporate more air into a liquid and can be used to make frothy foam on creamed soups. Be sure to completely immerse the blade in the food to prevent spattering.

MAKING STOCK

A stock is a well-flavored savory liquid made by simmering water for a few hours with meat and bones, seafood and bones or shells, or vegetables, along with aromatic ingredients such as spices, herbs, onions, and garlic. Most soups rely upon stock to give them body, and in this way stock is the primary source of a soup's consistency and flavor. The stock you make at home will yield the best-tasting soup with the fullest body.

With just a little planning, you can always have homemade stock on hand. Stock will keep in the refrigerator for only a few days but may be frozen for months. Whenever you trim poultry or seafood, save the scraps and freeze them for making a stock. If you have leftover shrimp, crab, or lobster shells, save and freeze them as well until you have enough to make stock. When you reach the amount needed for a recipe, take time on a weekend to make a pot of stock. The actual time of active work can be less than 20 minutes, and while the stock quietly simmers for a few hours, you will be able to turn your attention to other matters and be rewarded with plenty of stock on hand for future meals.

Before storing any stock in the refrigerator or freezer, make sure you allow it to cool down to room temperature first. Putting a large pot of hot stock into your refrigerator will warm up all the other foods. If you are planning to use the stock within 3 days, keep it covered in the refrigerator for that time. If you wish to have it on hand longer, store it in the freezer in 2- and 4-cup (16– and 32–fl oz/500-ml and 1-l) portions.

PREPARED BROTH

If you are in a hurry and prefer to buy prepared stock, generally called broth, choose a high-quality brand of canned, concentrated, or frozen broth. Look for prepared broths labeled "low sodium" to give you greater control over the seasoning in your final dish. It is easier to find a good ready-made chicken stock than a good beef or fish stock, but check with local gourmet markets and delicatessens. Chicken stock may be substituted for beef stock in a pinch, but the resulting soup will have less body and the flavors may not match as well. Bottled clam juice can be substituted for fish stock. Be sure to taste for salt before adding any salt to a soup made with prepared broth or clam juice, as these can be salty.

Shown opposite are the basic steps to making any stock:

1 **Making a bouquet garni:** A bouquet garni is a bundle of herbs added at the start of cooking to flavor a soup or stock. A traditional bouquet garni includes a few sprigs of parsley and thyme and a bay leaf and is usually tied in cheesecloth (muslin) to make the herbs easier to retrieve and discard at the end of cooking.

2 **Skimming the surface:** As the water for stock slowly heats, it draws from the ingredients fat and impurities that rise to the surface as a frothy foam. This foam should be skimmed away with a spoon, or the stock will be cloudy and its flavor less pure.

3 **Straining the stock:** After the stock has simmered for the specified time, the larger solids are strained out. Dampen a double thickness of cheesecloth (muslin), which helps trap fat and particles, use it to line a fine-mesh sieve, and then pour the stock through it into a large bowl.

4 **Degreasing the stock:** If you need to use a stock right away, skim the liquid fat from the surface with a large spoon or carefully blot up the fat with a folded paper towel. If you have more time, refrigerate the stock until well chilled, then use a slotted spoon to lift off and discard the solidified fat.

CHICKEN STOCK

4 fresh flat-leaf (Italian) parsley sprigs

1 fresh thyme sprig

1 bay leaf

6 lb (3 kg) chicken necks and backs

3 celery stalks

3 carrots, peeled

2 onions, root ends cut off, cut into halves

2 leeks, white and light green parts only, cleaned and sliced

Wrap the parsley, thyme, and bay leaf in a piece of cheesecloth (muslin) and secure the bundle with kitchen string to make a bouquet garni.

Combine the bouquet garni, chicken parts, celery, carrots, onions, and leeks in a large stockpot. Add enough cold water to just cover the ingredients (about 14 cups/3.5 l). Slowly bring to a boil over medium heat. Reduce the heat to as low as possible and let simmer, uncovered, for 3 hours, using a spoon or skimmer to regularly skim off the foam that rises to the surface. Taste and adjust the seasoning.

Strain the stock into a bowl through a colander or strainer lined with cheesecloth. Let cool at room temperature for about 1 hour, then cover and refrigerate for at least ½ hour or up to overnight. With a large spoon, remove the hardened fat from the surface and discard it.

Cover and refrigerate the stock for up to 3 days, or pour into airtight containers or zippered plastic freezer bags and freeze for up to 3 months. Makes about 3 qt (3 l).

BEEF STOCK

4 lb (2 kg) beef bones with some meat attached

4 fresh flat-leaf (Italian) parsley sprigs

1 fresh thyme sprig

1 bay leaf

2 large carrots, cut into 2-inch (5-cm) slices

1 large onion, cut into 2-inch (5-cm) slices

2 leeks, light green and dark green parts only, sliced into 2-inch (5-cm) chunks and rinsed carefully

Preheat the oven to 425°F (220°C). Place the beef bones in a large roasting pan. Place in the oven and roast until browned, about 1½ hours, stirring a few times to give the bones an even color.

Meanwhile, wrap the parsley, thyme, and bay leaf in a piece of cheesecloth (muslin) and secure the bundle with kitchen string to make a bouquet garni.

Remove the pan from the oven. Remove the bones and place them in a large stock-pot. Add about 3 cups (24 fl oz/750 ml) water to the roasting pan and place it over medium-high heat. Bring to a boil and deglaze the pan, stirring to scrape the browned bits from the pan's bottom. The water will become a rich brown color.

Transfer the deglazed juices from the roasting pan to the stockpot and add enough cold water (about 14 cups/3.5 l) to just cover the bones. Add the carrots, onion, and leeks and the bouquet garni.

Bring the mixture to a boil over medium heat, then reduce the heat to as low as possible. Let simmer, uncovered, for 4 hours, using a spoon or skimmer to regularly skim off the foam that rises to the surface. Taste and adjust the seasoning.

Turn off the heat and let the stock cool for ½ hour. Remove the bones and pour the stock into a large bowl through a fine-meshed strainer lined with cheesecloth. Let cool to room temperature, then cover and refrigerate for 2 hours.

With a large spoon, remove the hardened fat from the surface and discard it.

Line the strainer with cheesecloth, then pour the stock through again to make sure the stock is fat free. The stock should be clear. If not using immediately, pour into containers and refrigerate. The stock will keep for up to 3 days in the refrigerator or 3 months in the freezer. Makes 3 qt (3 l).

VEGETABLE STOCK

2 onions, thinly sliced

2 whole leeks, white and green parts, sliced and rinsed carefully

4 celery stalks with leaves, chopped

4 carrots, peeled and sliced lengthwise

1 red potato, diced

¼ lb (125 g) mushrooms, quartered

6 whole cloves garlic

8 fresh flat-leaf (Italian) parsley stems

2 bay leaves

8 whole peppercorns

Combine all the ingredients in a large stockpot. Add enough cold water to just cover the ingredients (about 10 cups/2.5 l). Bring to a boil over high heat, then reduce the heat to medium-low and let simmer, uncovered, for 1½ hours, using a spoon or skimmer to regularly skim off the foam that rises to the surface. Taste and adjust the seasoning.

Let the stock cool slightly. Strain through a fine-meshed strainer lined with cheesecloth (muslin) into a large bowl. Press on the vegetables with the back of a spoon to extract as much of the flavor as possible. Cool to room temperature and refrigerate. The stock will keep for up to 3 days in the refrigerator or 3 months in the freezer. Makes about 2 qt (2 l).

Variation Tip: This stock may be prepared using additional vegetables as desired, such as tomatoes, rutabagas, parsnips, turnips, or celery root (celeriac).

FISH STOCK

2 tablespoons vegetable oil

2 lb (1 kg) heads, skin, bones, and flesh of fresh white-fleshed fish, such as halibut or sea bass

1 onion, thinly sliced

2 carrots, unpeeled and cut into 2-inch (5-cm) pieces

6 fresh flat-leaf (Italian) parsley stems

2 celery stalks with leaves, cut into 2-inch (5-cm) pieces

1 bay leaf

10 white peppercorns

5 fresh dill sprigs

1 lemon, thinly sliced

In a large stockpot over low heat, warm the oil and sauté the fish parts for 2–3 minutes. Do not let them brown. Add all the remaining ingredients to the pot with enough cold water to just cover the ingredients (about 14 cups/3.5 l). Bring to a boil over medium-high heat. Reduce the heat to low and let simmer, uncovered, for 45 minutes, using a spoon or skimmer to regularly skim off the foam that rises to the surface. Taste and adjust the seasoning.

Strain the stock into a bowl through a colander or strainer lined with cheesecloth (muslin). Let cool for about 1 hour, then cover and refrigerate for at least ½ hour or overnight. With a large spoon, remove the hardened fat from the surface and discard it.

If the stock is not to be used at once, cover and refrigerate it for up to 3 days, or pour into airtight containers or zippered plastic freezer bags and freeze for up to 3 months. If frozen, it should be reboiled before using. Makes about 3 qt (3 l).

Variation Tip: This stock may also be made with shrimp, crab, or lobster shells, in place of or in addition to the fish parts.

GARNISHES AND ACCOMPANIMENTS

Garnishes are easy and attractive ways to give any bowl of soup added texture and flavor. They can be as simple as a sprinkle of grated Parmesan cheese or chopped herbs or more complex, such as a spoonful of pesto. You'll find garnishing ideas throughout this book, as well, including Basil Pesto (page 105), Garlic Croutons (page 72), Gremolata (page 81), Oregano Cream (page 40), Salsa Cream (page 86), and Sun-Dried Tomato Pesto (page 56). Following are two recipes that can add a little something extra to many meals. Cheese Croûtes can be floated on top of a soup or served as an accompaniment. Or, serving a soup with a side of Garlic Cheese Bread can be all you need to make a simple supper.

CHEESE CROÛTES

24 thin slices French or sourdough baguette

¼ cup (2 fl oz/60 ml) olive oil

⅓ cup (1½ oz/45 g) freshly grated Parmesan, Sonoma jack, or pecorino romano cheese

Preheat the oven to 375°F (190°C). Place the bread slices on a baking sheet and toast for 5 minutes.

Brush each toast on one side with the oil. Place the grated cheese on a flat plate and press the oiled side of each slice into the cheese to coat it evenly. Return the toasts to the baking sheet and bake for 5–7 minutes, or until the cheese is melted but not browned. Makes 24 toasts.

Variation Tip: To make sun-dried tomato croûtes, replace the ⅓ cup cheese with 3 tablespoons Sun-Dried Tomato Pesto (page 56) and omit the oil. Spread the slices evenly with the pesto and bake as directed.

Make-Ahead Tip: The croûtes can be prepared up to 1 week ahead and stored in an airtight container.

GARLIC CHEESE BREAD

½ cup (4 oz/125 g) unsalted butter, at room temperature

1 teaspoon whole-grain mustard

3 cloves garlic, minced

½ cup (2 oz/60 g) freshly grated Parmesan cheese

1 tablespoon finely chopped fresh basil

½ teaspoon finely chopped fresh thyme

⅛ teaspoon fresh oregano or pinch of dried oregano

Salt and freshly ground white pepper

1 large loaf fresh French or sourdough bread

In a small bowl, combine the butter and mustard and mix until well blended. Stir in the garlic, half of the Parmesan, the basil, thyme, oregano, and salt and white pepper to taste.

Preheat the oven to 400°F (200°C). Slice the bread in half lengthwise and spread each side with half of the herbed butter mixture. Sprinkle the two halves with the remaining Parmesan.

Slice the bread halves vertically in 2-inch (5-cm) slices, cutting three-fourths of the way down (by not cutting all the way through, the bread will still hold together). Wrap each of the bread halves in foil and close the ends tightly.

Place the loaves on a baking sheet and bake for 10 minutes. Remove the foil, return to the oven, and bake for another 5 minutes. Serve immediately. Makes 8 servings.

GLOSSARY

CHILES When working with any fresh chiles, avoid touching your eyes, mouth, or other sensitive areas. You may wish to use rubber gloves to protect your skin. Wash your hands and utensils immediately after working with chiles.

Here are a few very common chile types, used in the recipes in this book.

Ancho: A mild, dark reddish brown or brick red, squat-looking dried poblano chile about 4 inches (10 cm) long. They can pack a bit of heat along with their natural sweetness and are considered to make the best pure ground chili powder.

Chipotle: The smoked and dried version of jalapeños, chipotles are widely available canned with garlic, tomatoes, and vinegar and labeled "chipotles en adobo." They are moderately hot and have a distinctive smoky flavor.

Jalapeño: This bright green pepper, 1½ inches (4 cm) long, ranges from hot to very hot and is one of the most widely used in the United States. It is available canned or fresh and is sometimes seen in its bright red-ripe state.

Pasilla: Also called chile negro, this chile is dark, narrow, and wrinkled. About 6 inches (15 cm) long, pasillas are sweet and hot.

Thai: Small, thin green or red chiles, usually only about 1 inch (2.5 cm) long and very hot. Also known as bird chiles.

CHILI POWDER American chili powder combines ground dried chiles with other spices like cumin, garlic, oregano, and coriander.

CILANTRO Also known as coriander or Chinese parsley, cilantro is one of the most common fresh herbs used in Asian cooking and throughout the world. It has wide, flat leaves and a distinct flavor and aroma that livens up salads, salsas, and fish. Choose bright bunches of cilantro with fresh, crisp leaves and stems.

COCONUT MILK Available canned or bottled in Asian markets and large supermarkets, coconut milk is made by combining equal parts water and shredded fresh coconut and straining out the resulting milky liquid. Coconut milk is richly flavored, unsweetened but with a naturally sweet flavor, and is widely used in Southeast Asian and Pacific cooking. Don't confuse this with the very sweet coconut mixes for mixed drinks.

CUMIN This spice is characteristic in Mexican and Indian cooking and has a distinct aroma. Cumin is available in the spice section of supermarkets, either ground, or as light brown seeds that can be toasted and ground. It should be used sparingly to enhance the flavors of meats and vegetables, not overwhelm them.

FOOD MILL Used to purée cooked or very soft foods, a food mill looks like a sturdy plastic saucepan with a perforated bottom. A blade with a handle turns inside the mill to force food through the holes, but traps seeds, peels, and fibers. Food mills are more gentle than food processors and produce more even-textured purées.

GARLIC Fresh garlic is available all year-round. It should be creamy white or have a purplish red cast, and should be plump and firm, with its paperlike covering attached rather than shriveled. Store garlic in a cool, dry place with adequate ventilation (but not in the refrigerator).

GINGER Fresh ginger is a knobby-looking tuber with smooth, golden skin. Used throughout Chinese and Japanese cooking, ginger has become a common ingredient in American cooking as well. Ginger should be peeled first; then it may be shredded, grated, or cut into julienne strips. Do not substitute dried ginger for fresh.

JULIENNING Cutting food into long, thin matchstick strips called julienne. To julienne a vegetable such as a carrot, first cut the carrot into pieces of a desired length. Cut the pieces into strips, then stack the strips and slice them again to julienne them.

MATZO MEAL Unleavened bread called matzo is ground to make matzo meal. Traditionally eaten during the Jewish Passover holidays, matzo meal is available in Jewish markets and large supermarkets year-round.

PARMESAN CHEESE The authentic Italian Parmigiano-Reggiano comes from the Italian region of Emilia-Romagna, where it is strictly licensed and has been produced in much the same way for almost seven hundred years. The cheese should be straw yellow in color and have a crumbly, moist texture. Look for the words Parmigiano-Reggiano stamped on the rind of the cheese. Store the cheese wrapped in plastic in the refrigerator for up to 3 weeks. It is best to grate the Parmesan as needed for the best flavor.

PEPPER, WHITE White peppercorns are made from the same berry as black peppercorns, but are allowed to ripen longer before their skin is removed and the berry is dried. The resulting pepper is milder in flavor, but is generally used for aesthetic reasons rather than taste: White pepper blends visually into a light-colored dish or soup.

PORCINO MUSHROOM Also called cèpes, porcini are pale brown, smooth, and have a woodsy flavor. In the United States, porcini are most commonly found dried, although fresh mushrooms can be found in autumn.

SAUCEPAN A simple round pan usually with either straight or sloping sides. In general, saucepans range in size from 1 to 5 quarts (1 to 5 liters). Most useful is the 2-quart (2-liter) size. Traditional saucepans are twice as wide as they are high. This facilitates rapid evaporation, perfect for efficiently thickening soups. Straight-sided saucepans with high sides are also ideal for longer cooking, since the liquid will not boil away so quickly. The best materials for saucepans are anodized aluminum or aluminized steel.

SAUTÉING Taken from the verb "to jump" in French, *sauté* means to cook quickly in a small amount of fat. The pan should be preheated with the fat before adding foods so that they sear quickly, and there should be plenty of room in the pan so that foods don't get crowded and simmer in their own juices.

SESAME OIL Rich, dark amber-colored, and tasting like toasted sesame seeds, sesame oil should be used in small amounts. Don't confuse it with the clear-pressed sesame seed oil sold in health-food stores.

SHIITAKE MUSHROOM Dark brown shiitake mushrooms, common to Japanese and Chinese cuisines, are available fresh or dried almost year-round. They have tan undersides, a meaty texture, and a rich mushroom flavor. Soak all dried mushrooms in hot water before using and cut off the hard, knobby stem end. The soaking liquid can be strained and used to flavor soups and sauces.

SHRIMP, DEVEINING Some shrimp have a dark intestinal vein running through them that is removed primarily for aesthetic reasons. Shrimp deveining gadgets can be found in housewares stores, but a paring knife does a fine job. Make a shallow cut following the curve of the shrimp's back just down to the vein. Slip the tip of the knife under the vein, lift it, pull the vein away, and rinse the shrimp under cold water.

SKIMMER Designed to skim scum or foam from the top of simmering stocks, with a long handle and a large, shallow bowl of wire mesh or perforated metal.

STOCKPOT Also known as a soup pot, a stockpot is a high, narrow pot designed for minimal evaporation during long cooking. It is essential for making stock or cooking large quantities of soup. Stockpots are fitted with two looped handles for easy lifting and with tight-fitting lids. They should be made of heavy-gauge metal with good heft. Anodized aluminum or enameled steel are good choices because they absorb and transfer heat efficiently, clean up easily, and do not react with the acidity of wine or citrus juice. The smallest stockpots have an 8-quart (8-liter) capacity, but most cooks find stockpots with 10- to 12-quart (10- to 12-liter) capacities to be the most useful.

INDEX

APPLE PRESS
Sheridan House, 4th Floor
112-116A Western Road
Hove , East Sussex BN3 1DD
United Kingdom

WELDON OWEN INC.
Chief Executive Officer: John Owen
President: Terry Newell
Chief Operating Officer: Larry Partington
Vice President, International Sales: Stuart Laurence
Creative Director: Gaye Allen
Series Editor: Sarah Putman Clegg
Associate Editor: Heather Belt
Production Manager: Chris Hemesath
Production Assistant: Donita Boles
Studio Manager: Brynn Breuner
Photograph Editor: Lisa Lee

A Weldon Owen Production
Copyright © 2001 by Weldon Owen Inc. and
Williams-Sonoma Inc.

First Apple Press edition printed in 2002.

ISBN 1 84092 353 9

10 9 8 7 6 5 4 3 2 1

Set in Trajan, Utopia, and Vectora.

Color separations by Bright Arts Graphics
Singapore (Pte.) Ltd.
Printed and bound in Singapore by Tien Wah
Press (Pte.) Ltd.

A NOTE ON WEIGHTS AND MEASURES

All recipes include customary U.S. and metric measurements. Metric conversions are based on
a standard developed for these books and have been rounded off. Actual weights may vary.